about the editors

Andrew Chesler works as an artist and exhibits in New York City.

H. Amanda Robb works as a professional speechwriter.

Andrew and Amanda are married and co-authored *The Encyclopedia of American Family Names* (HarperCollins, 1995).

Sex, Sin & Mayhem
Notorious Trials of the 1990s

Uncover the stories behind recent headlines for 26 highly sensational, highly publicized celebrity trials and court battles, including: O. J. Simpson, Heidi Fleiss, the Menendez brothers, John and Lorena Bobbitt, Woody Allen/Mia Farrow custody case, Mike Tyson, Michael Jackson's settlement, Tonya Harding/Nancy Kerrigan conflict, Malice Green and William Kennedy Smith. Profiles set the scene, identify the principals, report the verdict and analyze the decision.

Edward W. Knappman • 5-1/2 x 8-1/2 • paperback • 210 pages • 35 photos • in print • ISBN 0-7876-0476-3

Great American Trials
From Salem Witchcraft to Rodney King

Two hundred historically significant, legally important and notorious trials that have captured the interest of the world are told through lively text, captivating photos and succinct coverage. Included are brief and accurate summaries of such trials as Dred Scott, Lizzy Borden, Leopold and Loeb, Teapot Dome, *Brown v. Board of Education*, Charles Manson, *Roe v. Wade*, Jim Bakker, Ted Bundy and Oliver North.

Edward W. Knappman • 7-1/4 x 9-1/4 • paperback • 872 pages • 175 photos • in print • ISBN 0-8103-9134-1

criminal, QUOTES

criminal
QUOTES

The 1,001
Most Bizarre
Things Ever
Said by
History's
Outlaws,
Gangsters,
Despots
and Other
Evil-doers

Edited by Andrew Chesler and H. Amanda Robb

VISIBLE
I N K

Detroit • New York • Toronto • London

Criminal Quotes

Published by Visible Ink Press®, a division of Gale Research

Visible Ink Press is a trademark of Gale Research

Most Visible Ink Press® books are available at special quantity discounts when purchased in bulk by corporations, organizations, or groups. Customized printings, special imprints, messages, and excerpts can be produced to meet your needs. For more information, contact Special Markets Manager, Gale Research, 835 Penobscot Bldg., Detroit, MI 48226. Or call 1-800-776-6265.

Art Director: Michelle DiMercurio
Typesetting by ExecuStaff Composition Services

Library of Congress Cataloging-in-Publication Data

Criminal quotes / edited by Andrew Chesler and H. Amanda Robb.
   p.   cm.
   Includes index.
   ISBN 0-7876-0937-4 (alk. paper)
   1. Criminals—Quotations. I. Chesler, Andrew. II. Robb, H. Amanda.
   PN6084.C7C75 1996
   364.3—dc20   96-25607
                                       CIP

---

contents

As we compiled these quotes—many of which took our breath away—we began wondering if a disclaimer could be attached to the title . . . something along the lines of *Criminal Quotes: You Know, Sometimes Nice People Publish a Not-So-Nice Book.* Such a thing wasn't possible, but we did want to offer a few words here in defense of our characters.

We think (and are told by our friends and family) that we are perfectly nice people. Everyone (okay, nearly everyone) who learned we were doing this project expressed some measure of surprise, saying things like, "You two seem so normal," or "I always thought of you as *decent.*" Well, we continue to think of ourselves as both normal and decent, just a regular couple with perhaps a slightly atypical appreciation of the absurd, bizarre, and outrageous.

For instance, like many other couples, we begin our day with cereal and the newspaper, but instead of discussing the day's events, we share our endless fascination with the words spewing from bad guys' mouths.

"Andrew," Amanda will say after quoting some heinous individual, "can you believe he said that?!"

"How about this one?" Andrew will counter with something he might find in the Metro section.

Amanda will nod her appreciation, then respond with a big outburst of criminal speech she's been saving for effect. Or, if it's a slow day for "good" bad quotes, she'll just ask for the coffee.

We've promised each other to give up this pastime when we have children.

Criminal Quotes is intended as dark humor—a laugh at the chilling, revealing, and simply peculiar things that criminals say. Indeed, every person quoted in this book has been indicted as a criminal by a judicial body or by history.

We are, of course, well aware that many of these people have been convicted of committing heinous crimes, and we in no way wish to make light of their wrongdoing or of the suffering of their victims. We very sincerely hope readers take *Criminal Quotes* in the vein in which it was conceived and compiled.

No book is ever published by authors alone. For enabling *Criminal Quotes* to reach your bookshelf, we'd like to thank a few people who are at least as nice as we are: our editor Becky Nelson, associate editor Dean Dauphinais, our agent Ed Knappman, and the librarians at the New York Public Library.

criminal QUOTES

[Adolf Hitler] was a great man and a real conqueror whose name would never be forgotten.
—Idi Amin, 1970s Ugandan general/dictator.

> The Ford has got ever [sic] other car out there skinned and even if my business hasen't [sic] been strictly legal it don't hurt eny [sic] thing to tell you what a fine car you got in the V8.
> —Clyde Barrow, of the "Bonnie and Clyde" bank robbing duo, in a letter sent to Henry Ford, head of the Ford Motor Company, in 1934.

A complete gentleman. . . . There was nobody in the world—I don't give a goddamn about your presidents, your kings, or whatever—nobody compared with Frank Costello. He was a dignified man; class just leaked out of him.
—Mickey Cohen, mobster, speaking about famous mobster Frank Costello.

Look, this was a great guy!
—Mickey Cohen, mobster, on his underling, Johnny Stompanato, whose specialty was blackmailing rich women, including Lana Turner, by secretly filming their trysts with him. Stompanato was stabbed to death by Turner's daughter.

> . . . .You have a wonderful car. Been driving one for three weeks. It's a treat to drive one. Your slogan should be, Drive a Ford and watch the other cars fall behind you. I can make any other car take a Ford's dust.
> —John Dillinger, infamous bank robber of the 1920s and '30s, in a letter sent to Henry Ford, head of the Ford Motor Company, in 1934.

Like a rising star you appeared before our wondering eyes, you performed miracles to clear our minds and, in a world of skepticism and desperation, gave us faith.
—Joseph Goebbels, Nazi propaganda minister, in a letter to Nazi leader Adolf Hitler.

It was granted me for many years to live and work under
the greatest son whom my nation has brought forth in
the thousand years of its history.
—Rudolf Hoess, deputy leader of the Nazi Party, speaking of Adolf Hitler, after the Nazis
lost World War II.

Just like you, Nick, he's a real gangster, always for the underdog.
—Dave Iacovetti, mobster, talking with Nick Scarfo, Bruno/Scarfo crime family boss, about Gambino crime
family boss John Gotti.

There is a big difference between your Mafiya in the West
and ours. The Cosa Nostra are noble people. Who could
be against well-organized societies? But our Mafiya are
not organized, at least not as they should be. That's why
everything is in disorder here. Nobody knows whom to
obey. When there is no order . . . people cannot live
normal lives.
—Ted Kasyanov, Russian strongman arrested in Russia for murder and kidnapping.

These Sicilian Mafioso will run into a wall, put their head
in a bucket of acid for you if they're told to, not because
they're hungry but because they're disciplined. They've
been brought up from birth over there to show respect
and honor, and that's what these punks over here don't
have. Once they're told to get someone, that person hasn't
a chance. They'll get him if they have to bust into his
house in the middle of the night, shoot him, bite him, eat
him, suck the blood out of his throat. They'll get him
because they were told to do it.
—Vincent Teresa, confessed Mafia member on the Sicilian Mafia.

adventure

What a thrill that will be if I have to die in the electric chair. It will be the supreme thrill. The only one
I haven't tried.
—Albert Howard Fish, sadomasochistic child killer, upon learning that he would be
sent to death in the electric chair. He even helped the guards affix the electrodes to
his legs.

The year 1990 started out with a bang for me. In its first week I was involved in planning to kill one of New Jersey's biggest drug dealers. . . .
—George Fresolone, member of the Bruno/Scarfo crime family, on being fully involved in the upper echelon of the Mafia.

advice

Gentlemen, it is much easier in many cases to go into combat with a company than to suppress an obstructive population of low cultural level, or to carry out executions or to haul away people or to evict crying and hysterical women.
—Heinrich Himmler, Nazi, Reichsführer-SS, head of the Gestapo and Waffen-SS, and minister of the interior of Nazi Germany, speaking to an SS regiment.

Bobby, watch your ass. Don't trust anybody but me and the boys.
—Jimmy Hoffa, Teamsters leader imprisoned for fraudulent use of union pension funds and jury tampering, referring to himself and his underlings, to fellow inmate Bobby Baker, a former secretary to the majority of the U.S. Senate, on whom to trust in prison.

Treat the sucker right. He is paying your salary. His stupidity is our income. You must never insult him, just cheat him with a smile.
—Arnold Rothstein, illegal gambling impresario, talking about people who are indebted to him.

age

I'm really getting too old for this sort of thing.
—William Miner, outlaw train and stagecoach robber, after he was arrested for the last of his many robberies, speaking to a deputy.

aggravation

I can't stand squealers! Hit the guy!
—Albert Anastasia, Mafia executioner, speaking to his hit men after finding out that Brooklyn ito good samaritan with no mob ties, Arnold Schuster, had alerted the police that bank robber Willie Sutton was in town. Schuster was subsequently "hit," meaning killed.

altruism

The poorest man in Uganda is General Amin. It is better for me to be poor and the people rich.
—Idi Amin, 1970s Ugandan general/dictator. His reign of brutality, torture, and mass murder left as many as 300,000 people dead or missing and the vast majority of Ugandans impoverished.

ambition

That is my ambition, to have killed more people—more helpless people than any man or woman who has ever lived.
—Jane Toppan, Massachusetts nurse who confessed to killing 31 people, speaking to the court at her trial.

animal rights

Take that! No horse can kill a pal of mine and get away with it.
—"Two Gun" Louis Alterie, Chicago bootleg-era gunman, to the horse that threw and killed his friend Morton. Alterie shot the horse to death with his two .38s.

I like de kits and boids. I'll beat up any guy dat gets gay wit' a kit or boid in my neck of de woods.
—Edward "Monk" Eastman, a.k.a. Edward Osterman, New York City crime boss of the late-19th and early-20th centuries. Eastman's passions were cats and pigeons.

I wanted the pleasure of shooting something new.
—Michel Henriot, French fox breeder who killed his wife in order to collect her life insurance policy. He was known to shoot animals just to watch them die.

anticipation

I been waiting for this day for at least eight years. You're gonna be on top if I have to kill everybody for you. With you there, that's the only way we can have any peace and make the real money.
—Albert Anastasia, a.k.a. the "Mad Hatter of Crime," Mafia executioner, expressing his joy to "Lucky" Luciano after Luciano told him he was planning to destroy two other Mafia factions and increase his power.

She's not dead yet but she soon will be.
—Louisa May Merrifield, a British woman who had already been to prison on fraud charges, speaking about the elderly woman she had been caring for and later poisoned to death.

I feel keyed up as if I was planning a surprise party. So next time I write in the diary mother will be dead. How odd, yet how pleasing.
—Pauline Parker, 16-year-old New Zealand girl who plotted her mother's death so she herself could be alone with her 15-year-old girlfriend, Juliet Hume.

apology

I'm sorry I killed five people, okay?
—Gary Alan Walker, rapist and murderer, confessing to the police.

arrogance

I know what's best for foreign policy and national security.
—Aldrich Ames, CIA agent secretly working for the KGB, while in prison for treason.

The bullet hasn't been made that can kill me.
—Jack "Legs" Diamond, lifetime criminal involved in drug smuggling, robbery, and murder, who survived numerous gun battles and injuries, but was ultimately shot to death by gangsters reputed to be working for the gangster Dutch Schultz in 1931.

If they want to call me boss of bosses, that's all right.
—Carmine Galante, a.k.a. "Mr. Lilo," mobster in the Bonnano crime family.

I'm an intelligent man. I didn't think you'd catch me.
—Edward Lester Gibbs, a student at Franklin and Marshall College, to the college president, confessing to the murder of a college secretary.

Why do you have to know?
—Fanya Kaplan, Russian woman who shot and seriously wounded Vladimir Ilyich Lenin, the Russian revolutionary and founder of Bolshevism, when asked why she shot Lenin.

When I die, what a great artist will be lost.
—Nero, fifth emperor of Rome.

Now that everyone is happy [in Iran], I allow my coronation to take place.
—Mohammad-Reza Pahlavi, the Shah of Iran, who organized Savak, a brutal secret police renowned for its torture techniques.

the arts

When I hear the word "culture," I slip back the safety catch of my revolver.
—Hanns Johst, Nazi poet laureate and playwright, from his play *Schlageter.*

attitude

I never forgive.
—Queen Christina, 17th-century Swedish monarch who was never noted for hesitating before ordering an execution, at six years of age.

You'd probably be like me if you had the nerve.
—Harry Pierpont, bank-robbing cohort of John Dillinger, to the prosecutor at his murder trial.

bets

I bet I kill a man today before you do.
—William Bonney, a.k.a. "Billy the Kid," legendary outlaw of the Old West, to his companion, minutes before killing a man in a bar.

the big picture

It was only one life. What is one life in the affairs of a state?
—Benito Mussolini, fascist Italian leader, after the car he was riding in hit and killed a child.

blame

It was *her* idea, not mine. Why should I forfeit my life alone? Why not the woman, too?
—Michel Eyraud, French murderer, casting blame on his accomplice and lover, prostitute Gabrielle Bompard, for the death of their victim in 1888.

Here I was, making [a] grand a year knocking over those tin-can state banks. But that wasn't enough for you. Now we've got heat smeared all over us. And you got me into this mess!
—George "Machine Gun" Kelly, bank robber and kidnapper of the 1920s and '30s, to his wife, after apparently tiring of being on the run from the law after Kelly and his wife kidnapped a rich Texas oilman.

She shouldn't have got in the way of the bullet.
—Giuseppe Zangara, Italian-born gunman who some say worked for the Mafia. Zangara shot and killed Chicago Mayor Anton J. Cermak, but may have been aiming for President Franklin Roosevelt, who was standing at Cermak's side at the time. Zangara is referring to a woman who was hit by one of his bullets.

boasts

I'm still able to do my own killings.
—Benny Binion, Nevada gambling king jailed for tax evasion.

I can do that standing on my head.
—Leo Vincent Brothers, St. Louis killer hired by mobster Al Capone to kill newsman Jake Lingle in 1930, after learning his sentence would be fourteen years in jail.

I'm no average killer.
—Raymond Martinez Fernandez, a.k.a. Charles Martin, a killer who found his victims in the lonely hearts column of the newspaper. He was married to Martha Julie Beck—together they were known as "The Lonely Hearts Killers"—and admitted to killing seventeen people in order to rob them of their savings.

If I put up a poster for every seven Poles shot, the forests of Poland would not be sufficient to manufacture the paper for such posters.
—Hans Frank, Nazi governor general of Poland during World War II.

I can frighten or buy 99 out of every 100 men.
—Louisiana Governor Huey "The Kingfish" Long.

The strangling itself was quite easily accomplished.
—Herbert Leonard Mills, a young British poet who volunteered to write the story of his discovery of the body of a murdered woman for a London newspaper. In his account he bragged that he actually mesmerized the woman with his poetry, seduced her, and then killed her.

```
I shot the asshole three times. The
papers didn't say so but I'm telling
you it was me, with another soldier,
who went into the apartment and boom,
boom, I shot him three times. . . .
They say he's . . . still got two [bul-
lets in his head] and they can't get
them out. . . . But he'll remain crip-
pled. . . . It's worse than being dead.
```
—Paolo Violi, Italian-born heir to the Cotroni crime family who was sentenced to jail for contempt of court, bragging about how he avenged an attempt on his life by a rival.

She should have been along that time in the New York
Central Building when I knocked off that guy Maramaneza
[sic]. Now that was a honey.
—Bo Weinberg, underling to mob boss Dutch Schultz, recounting bragging to his
girlfriend about killing Salvatore Maranzano, another mobster, who Weinberg
called "Maramaneza."

boredom

I hadn't anything else to do, that's why I went around
bumping off cops.
—Francis "Two-Gun" Crowley, bank robber convicted of killing a shopkeeper and
a policeman.

I was losing anyway. Let's go. I have nothing better to do.
—Roy Gardner, train robber and escape artist dubbed Public Enemy Number One, to
the police as they arrested him during a poker game.

boy talk

Communism. The KGB.
—Aldrich Ames, CIA agent secretly working for the KGB, when asked what he and his
father talked about when Ames was a boy.

business as usual

They got to make a buck. They're human, too. Treat 'em
nice. Then, if you get into trouble you may be able to do
business with 'em.
—Danny Ahearn, New York City-based killer of the 1930s and '40s who was twice tried
for murder, on the subject of professional assassins.

I think we've executed him.
—Syrian President Hafez Asad, upon being asked what had become of a security aid
to the previous leader of Syria.

Seek wealth, it's good.
—Ivan Boesky, Wall Street financier convicted of securities fraud.

The only thing we have to sell is fear.
—William E. "Billy" Dauber, a Chicago-based mob hit man, on being a gangster.

No one will walk out of Auschwitz! There is only one way they will leave—through the smokestacks!

—Karl Adolf Eichmann, Nazi SS leader who oversaw the extermination of millions of people in concentration camps during World War II, replying to the idea that it would be better to use the remaining living prisoners as a way of negotiating with the soon-to-be-victorious Allied forces.

The way they change sides back and forth makes me wanna puke. . . . I know that, someday, sometime, they're gonna say, 'Enough of this shit,' working for the feds for lousy pay . . . and they're gonna go into private practice defending us. They're gonna get fucking rich . . . They pay their dues working for the government, then they squeeze our balls because of all the connections they've developed.

—Joe N. Gallo, consigliere of the Gambino crime family, on the subject of lawyers.

My profession was robbing banks, knocking off payrolls, and kidnapping rich men. I was good at it.

—Alvin "Creepy" Karpis, freelance criminal.

What the hell, it was just a business like any other. They performed a service and got paid for it. That's all there was to it.

—Charles "Lucky" Luciano, mobster-founder of the national crime syndicate—the network of criminal groups that controls organized crime—when asked how he felt about being part of Murder, Inc., the organization that killed hundreds of people.

If a man makes a living with his hands I would destroy his hands. You make your living with your face, so I will destroy your face. I'll get you where it hurts the most! I'll cut you up and I'll get you mother and your daughter too. . . . That's my business!

—Johnny Stompanato, Hollywood mobster, whose specialty was blackmailing rich women by secretly filming their trysts with him, here threatening the actress Lana Turner. Stompanato was stabbed to death by Turner's daughter.

. . . if they gave me a contract to hit you and I was an outsider, after I would hit you and I would come to collect the money, they would say, "Yes, come on, we will go down the street and get it," and that would be the end. They would leave me in the trunk, too.

—Vincent Teresa, confessed Mafia member.

business opportunities

We mostly did Italian weddings. We cleaned out the house while the people were at the church.

—Peter Bianco, soldier in the Violi crime family, on the types of burglaries they favored.

We had already made our investment in the boardinghouse, and it was simply a matter of doing the right thing with it.

—Ada Everleigh, a late-19th-century madam, known together with her sister Minna as "The Scarlet Sisters," on the decision to turn their respectable boarding house into a brothel.

I was elated because the job was done and I was gonna become one of *them* and share in the profits. It was something that since I was a kid I had dreamed of.

—Raymond Ferritto, a professional burglar who planted the bomb that killed Danny Greene, a Cleveland, Ohio, mobster.

Legit rackets, there ain't no sense to 'em—you've got to wait for your dough.

—Owen Victor Madden, Liverpool-born teenage gang leader and, later, successful 1930s mobster.

It's an unbelievable business. . . . It's even mostly legal.

—Richie Martino, Gambino crime family member, on the phone-sex business he set up for the Gambino mob.

Nobody ever put over big-time religion here like I did. I broke this town spiritually by spending five, six thousand dollars a week on advertising.

—Carl Thomas Patten, revivalist preacher who bilked many of his followers of their savings and was ultimately imprisoned for grand theft.

celebrities

I could whack out a couple of those guys. Lawford, that Martin prick, and I could take the nigger and put his other eye out.

—Johnny Formosa, Mafia hit man, expressing anger that Hollywood hadn't done more to help the mob. Peter Lawford, Dean Martin, and Sammy Davis, Jr.—who had lost an eye in a car accident—were all members of the Hollywood "Rat Pack," a group of high-living actors in the 1950s and '60s.

Let's show 'em. Let's show 'em. Those f— Hollywood fruitcakes that they can't get away with it as if nothing's happened. . . . Let's get [Sinatra]!
—Johnny Formosa, Mafia hit man, expressing anger that Hollywood hadn't done more to help the mob. Singer/actor Frank Sinatra was a member of Hollywood's "Rat Pack."

I'll mutilate you! I'll hurt you so that you'll be so repulsive you'll have to hide forever!
—Johnny Stompanato, Hollywood mobster, whose specialty was blackmailing rich women by secretly filming their trysts with him, here threatening the actress Lana Turner. Stompanato was stabbed to death by Turner's daughter.

challenges

Are you hiding behind a shield? Is it bulletproof? Are we going to have a shooting match? It's just what I like!
—Christopher Craig, teenage British robber and murderer, shouting to the police during a gunfight at a London warehouse in 1952.

The chances that you took was just part and parcel— they made it more invigorating, they added to the challenge of it.
—Mickey Cohen, mobster, speaking euphemistically about murder, which he called "giving a guy a deal."

To me it was like having a glass of wine. It didn't mean a thing. I killed him and there was no remorse that I killed a man because I was brought up all through my life believing in those . . . things or hurdles you just had to overcome.
—Raymond Ferritto, a professional burglar who planted the bomb that killed Danny Greene, a Cleveland, Ohio, mobster.

Produce your corpses!
—Henri Desire Landru, a.k.a. "Bluebeard," French mass murderer who, according to conservative estimates, killed 20 women, responding to the prosecution at his trial in 1922. The corpses could not be produced because Landru had cut them into small pieces and burned them in his fireplace.

charity

I don't think I commit any sin in robbing a person of
quality because I keep generally pretty close to the text
"Feed the hungry and send the rich away empty."
—Richard Dudley, 17th-century British murderer and robber whose victims were from
the upper classes.

childhood

Other kids are brought up nice and sent to Harvard or
Yale. Me? I was brought up like a mushroom.
—Frank Costello, Mafia boss originally from Calabria, Italy, on being an immigrant.

choices

Either you're gonna get faded outta the picture or you're
gonna have to go to war. That's disorganized crime. Going out and stealing.
—Dominick Montiglio, former Gambino crime family associate.

There is a mysticism about men. There is a quiet confidence. You look a man in the eye and you know he's got
it—brains. This guy has got it. If he doesn't, Nixon has
made a bum choice.
—Richard Nixon, U.S. president, on his selection of Spiro Agnew as vice president.
Agnew later pleaded nolo contendere to income tax evasion charges and resigned.

colleagues

If you're writing a book about how
nice a guy Frank was, don't put too
much in there about the twenties.
—Anonymous associate of mobster Frank Costello.

Phil dumps the bum out and then brings out some gas
and dumps it all over the guy. Then he lights the guy up
and watches him burn. "Puggy makes a nice fire, don't
he?" Phil says. "Yeah," I says. Whattaya gonna say to
somethin' like that? Huh? Phil is nuts.
—Abe Reles, a paid killer for Murder, Inc., on the methods of another hit man, "Pittsburgh Phil," whose real name was Harry Strauss.

I don't trust Legs. He's nuts. He gets excited and starts
pulling a trigger like another guy wipes his nose.
—Dutch Schultz, a.k.a. Arthur Flegenheimer, New York mobster, talking about rival
gangster "Legs" Diamond.

(small) comforts

I'm only going to shoot, and I'm a bad shot.
—Rodolfo Fierro, lieutenant of Mexican revolutionary Pancho Villa, before shooting
299 out of 300 prisoners.

We only killed our own.
—Bugsy Siegel, mobster and part of Murder, Inc., stating one of the guiding principles
of mob life.

community

I hope they send me to Alcatraz. All my friends are there.
—Edward Wilhelm Bentz, bank robber who collaborated with other famous bank robbers, such as John Dillinger and Harvey Bailey. His wish was ultimately granted.

I went back to Spofford about eight times after that. Mostly
for robberies. . . . I had done so many. You know, after
knowing all my friends were there I was not at all afraid
of it. It was like a country club and I was like a regular.
—Mike Tyson, heavyweight champion boxer convicted of rape, on his childhood life
of crime and the juvenile center to which he was sent.

comparisons

Am I to resort to suppression, like the Shah?
—Ayatollah Ruhollah Khomeini, Iranian religious leader and virtual dictator, who im-
posed Muslim fundamentalist law and condoned taking of U.S. hostages. The Shah's
reign was also noted for the torture techniques of his secret police.

People here are much easier to cheat here than in Italy.
—Giacomo Luppino, don of the Hamilton, Ontario, mob.

Only Capone kills like that!
—George "Bugs" Moran, Chicago mobster of the 1920s and '30s, speculating to news-
men that Al Capone's gangsters were the killers of seven of his men in the "St.
Valentine's Day Massacre" of 1929. When asked who he thought was responsible for
the killings, Capone replied, "The only man who kills like that is Bugs Moran."

The place was like an asylum and the lunatics were everywhere. They were in charge.
—Benito Mussolini, fascist Italian leader, on the aftermath of an attempt on Hitler's life.

When Nixon was President and Leader of the Free World, he found that firmness paid.
—Richard Nixon, U.S. president, who made a habit of referring to himself in the third person, at a private dinner party with Chinese officials shortly after the massacre at Tiananmen Square. Nixon was president in 1970 when the National Guard fired on and killed Kent State University students who were protesting the Vietnam War.

When you get a job with the telephone company or maybe even Mays Department Store, they take something out of every paycheck for taxes, right? And every year, it gets to be a little more. Now, people gripe, but they pay those taxes, Woody. They pay it, because if they don't, the government is going to tromp down on them. It's a fact of life. Now why, you may ask, does the government have a right to make you pay taxes? Well, it's a fair question. The answer to that question, Woody, is that you pay taxes for the right to live and work and make money at a legit business. Does that make sense? . . . Well, it's the exact same situation. You did a crooked job in Brooklyn. You worked hard and you earned a lot of money. Now you got to pay your taxes on it just like in the straight world. Because we let you do it. We're the government. That's why I say we're always in the picture.
—Carmine "The Snake" Persico, Colombo crime family boss, from a taped conversation, explaining the facts of doing business with the Mafia to "Woody," an unknown swindler who had just pulled a half-million-dollar heist on Mays department store.

I'm not the kind of man you are, robbing widows and orphans.
—Harry Pierpont, bank robbing cohort of John Dillinger, to the prosecutor at his murder trial.

We were a single body, bandits, police and Mafia, like the Father, the Son, and the Holy Ghost.
—Gaspare Pisciotta, a Mafia lieutenant who killed his bandit-uncle because the uncle was plotting to overthrow the Mafia in Sicily, Italy, in a statement to the police.

Look what happened to Germany in the 1930s. The dignity
of man was subordinated to the powers of Nazism. . . .
Those are the forces that this can evolve into.
—James G. Watt, Ronald Reagan's interior secretary, comparing Nazis and environmentalists. In 1996 Watt pleaded guilty to a misdemeanor charge of trying to influence a
federal grand jury.

I could understand where she was coming from.
—James William Wilson, whose pistol attack on the children and workers of an elementary school in
South Carolina left two children dead and nine people injured, on the motives of Laurie Dann, who as-
saulted an Illinois school in a similar manner.

complaints

. . . I am convinced that the Prince of Darkness will be
taxed to devise a torture I would regard as merely an
annoyance after my conditioning by the sovereign State
of California.
—Caryl Chessman, robber and sex offender who spent 12 years on death row before
being put to death in 1960.

Bob Kennedy won't stop today until he puts us all in jail
all over the country.
—Michelino Clemente, Profaci crime family member, complaining about U.S. Attorney
General Robert F. Kennedy's crackdown on organized crime.

You are going to keep me locked up in Dayton, Ohio? I'm
not a priest.
—Slobodan Milosevic, president of Serbia, who endorses the concept of "ethnic cleans-
ing," or murder, of Muslims in the former Yugoslavia, joking about the location of the
talks to end the war in Bosnia and Herzegovina.

Did you see poor Jerry O'Connor's face in the funeral
home? It was all blown off. Nothing left to it. . . . That
Capone kills like a beast in the jungle.
—Charles Dion O'Bannion, Chicago North Side mob boss and rival of Al Capone's,
on Capone's way of killing off his rivals.

There goes my couple of thousand that he owes me.
—Joseph Valachi, a henchman in the Genovese crime family, before having a Bureau
of Narcotics informant killed.

compliments

Around this room, we have gathered the very best people of our brotherhood. But it is a great shame that the majority of us are seriously addicted.
—Anonymous Russian drug smuggler, speaking at a "colleague's" funeral.

Isn't he a brainy swine?
—Ian Brady, 28-year-old Englishman, after bludgeoning a man to death.

You'd make a good corpse.
—Louis Dwight Brookins, killer who lured young women to desolate areas and killed them, to a potential victim who escaped.

confessions

I guess I did it. No one else was there.
—Dr. Arnold Asher Axilrod, Minneapolis dentist who drugged, raped, and, in one case, murdered his patients.

Once I stabbed her once, I couldn't stop . . . I keep hitting her and hitting her with that knife . . . she keep bleeding from the throat . . . I hit her and hit her and hit her. . . .
—Albert Henry DeSalvo, a.k.a. "The Boston Strangler," confessing to the murder of a 23-year-old graduate student.

I know exactly what I was doing at the time of the murders, and it was right. . . . Nothing could stop me from murdering them.
—Michael Edward Drabing, Illinois man who modeled himself on Charles Manson and killed three people as they were relaxing in their home in 1976.

I have brought disgrace on the college.
—Edward Lester Gibbs, a student at Franklin and Marshall College, to the college president, confessing to the murder of a college secretary.

That's us.
—Patrick Kearney and David Hill, upon walking into a police station and pointing to their own photographs posted on the wall. Kearney and Hill were a homosexual couple responsible for the California "trash bag" murders, a series of killings in which the victims' bodies were found wrapped in trash bags.

By the way, I also poisoned my father in law, and I killed
my husband too.
—Christa Ambros Lehmann, a German housewife and murderer, who claimed she only
intended to make her friend sick with poisoned chocolates, but ended up killing her.

conflict

My will was innocent, but my body was compelled.
—Edward Dennis, 18th-century British executioner who robbed a store.

congeniality

He was always unpopular. He would kill a friend.
—Anonymous crime figure discussing mobster "Legs" Diamond.

conscience

I have never suffered from the qualms of conscience. I
have had no regrets—except when I was caught. I am not
really sorry I was a criminal.
—May Churchill, a.k.a. "Chicago May," Irish-born bank robber who teamed up with
the notorious professional criminal Eddie Guerin to pull off the 1901 robbery of the
American Express office in Paris.

. . . . All I know is that I went to bed that night and I slept.
—Raymond Ferritto, a professional burglar, talking about the night he planted the bomb
that killed Danny Greene, a Cleveland, Ohio, mobster.

. . . because I had been ordered to kill these 80 intern-
ees in this way, as I have told you. Anyway, this is how
I was brought up.
—Josef Kramer, a.k.a. "The Beast of Belsen," commander of the Nazi concentration
camps at Birkenau and Bergen-Belsen, when asked whether he had any qualms about
his work.

I've killed a dozen men myself, but I was never bothered
in my sleep until I killed that girl.
—Jason Labreu, American outlaw of the 1880s who drowned a young girl.

. . . even as far as God's concerned. . . . I'm not doing
anything wrong.
—Philip Leonetti, Philadelphia-based Mafia underboss.

In my lifetime I have murdered 21 human beings. I have committed thousands of burglaries, robberies, larcenies, arsons and last but not least I have committed sodomy on more than 1,000 male human beings. For all of these things I am not the least bit sorry. I have no conscience so that does not worry me, I don't believe in man, God nor Devil. I hate the whole damned human race including myself.

—Carl Panzram, misanthropic mass murderer writing in his autobiography. Initially sentenced to 25 years in prison, Panzram killed again while incarcerated and was executed in 1930.

consequences

Hell, the worst I can get is life.

—Dave Berman, bootlegger and bank robber arrested for kidnapping, speaking to a detective who was interrogating him.

That's what made me hate, really, fuckin' Paul. You, ya, you couldn't even get a fuckin' ham sandwich [from him]. . . . He sold the borágta [family] out for [a] fuckin' construction company.

—John Gotti, boss of the Gambino crime family, on his predecessor, Paul Castellano, whose murder Gotti arranged.

I had it coming—and more. I couldn't have beefed if the judge had given me the hot seat.

—Joseph Kadlecek, a factory worker who murdered a young woman. He made this remark after the judge had sentenced him to 60 years in prison.

No man drinks beer with me. I don't like beer.

—John Ringo, gunslinger of the American Old West, after inviting a man to have a drink with him in a saloon. Ringo apparently shot the man to death because he ordered beer instead of whiskey.

Sometimes things go bad. Sometimes, people—they get shot.

—Kenny Vu, member of a Chinese gang.

(small) consideration

Do you still want to continue this?
—Jack Henry Abbott, murderer turned novelist turned murderer, to the waiter he had
just fatally stabbed through the heart outside a New York City restaurant in 1981.

conspiracy theories

**It's against the fucking rules to kill a cop, so now we're
going to kill the president.**
—Jimmy "The Weasel" Fratianno, Mafia boss turned informer, on the subject of President John F. Kennedy's assassination.

**Listen, honey, if it wasn't for me your boyfriend wouldn't
even be in the White House.**
—Momo Salvatore "Sam" Giancana, Cosa Nostra overlord of the Chicago area, to one
of John F. Kennedy's mistresses, Judy Campbell.

**Kennedy's not going to make it to the election. He's
going to be hit.**
—Santo Trafficante, Tampa, Florida, Mafia boss, on President John F. Kennedy's
reelection prospects.

We shouldn't have killed John. We should have killed Bobby.

—Santo Trafficante, Tampa, Florida, Mafia boss, to his lawyer, on the assassination of President John F.
Kennedy. The "Bobby" Trafficante was referring to was Kennedy's brother, Robert, the United States attorney general.

**Mark my word, this man Kennedy is in trouble, and he
will get what's coming to him.**
—Santo Trafficante, Tampa, Florida, Mafia boss, referring to United States Attorney
General Robert Kennedy's persecution of the Mafia.

**See what Kennedy done. With a Kennedy, a guy should
take a knife, like one of them other guys, and stab and
kill the fucker, where he is now. Someone should kill the
fucker. I mean it. This is true. Honest to God. It's about
time to go. But I'll tell you something. I hope I get a
week's notice. I'll kill. Right in the fuckin' White House.
Somebody's got to get rid of this fucker.**
—Willie Weisburg, "business associate" of Philadelphia Mafia boss Angelo Bruno, discussing the Kennedys.

contempt

Even when they've been taken, they'll come back for
more. They're the sort of hick you can sting twice in the
same place and get away with it.
—The Crying Kid, 1870s con artist, on his victims.

correction

They say I used a piece of Henry II furniture. I don't
know how old the furniture was. In any case I didn't hit
them. I just destroyed them psychologically.
—Klaus Barbie, a.k.a. "The Butcher of Lyons," a Nazi, on his methods for interrogating
the French.

I read your statements about me poisoning people with
arsenic. That's ridiculous! If I had used arsenic, my patients would have died hard deaths. I could not bear to
see them suffer. When I kill anyone, they go to sleep and
never wake up.
—Jane Toppan, Massachusetts nurse who confessed to killing 31 people, speaking to
the authorities.

correspondence

Don't worry about me honey, for that won't help any, and
besides I am having a lot of fun.
—John Dillinger, infamous bank robber of the 1920s and '30s, from a letter to his
sister, written while he was on the run from the police.

You can send my mail to Canon City (Prison) until next
month. After that you can send it to hell.
—John "Jack" Gilbert Graham, who sabotaged the flight his mother was on, killing
her and 43 others in the process, telling his wife where to send his mail. Graham
was to be executed.

Don't ask me where I got it! But it
could possibly be very valuable.
—Joe Tom Meador, American soldier in World War II, in a letter to his parents. He had been ordered to guard the "Quedlinburg Treasure," a priceless trove of medieval artworks, but mailed them
home instead.

I AM VERY MUCH SURPRISED WHAT I HAVE BEEN
READING IN THE NEWSPAPERS BETWEEN YOU AND
YOUR DARLING WIFE. REMEMBER YOU HAVE A DE-
CENT WIFE AND CHILDREN. YOU SHOULD BE VERY
HAPPY. REGARDS TO ALL. WILLIE MOORE.
—Willie Moretti, a.k.a. Willie Moore, New Jersey Syndicate boss, in a telegram to Frank
Sinatra after reading newspaper reports that Sinatra was seeking to divorce his wife.
Moretti, meanwhile, was shot to death by fellow mobsters because they were afraid that
his deteriorating mental health, which was brought about by the effects of syphilis, would
cause him to reveal mob secrets.

April Fool.
—The Reno Brothers—Frank, John Simeon, and William, a.k.a. "The Reno Gang." They left
this message on the wall of their Council Bluffs, Missouri, jail cell after their April 1, 1868,
escape. The Renos were a notorious gang believed to have been the first ever to rob a train.

. . . though you now contemplate prosecuting me, you
will probably have to prosecute my corpse.
—Cornelius Van Heerden, 22-year-old South African railroad worker who killed five
people and shot six others before killing himself in 1931, in a letter to the police.

criticism

This country is a mess! That man is not your President!
He is not a public servant! He is not a public servant!
—Lynette "Squeaky" Fromme, a member of Charles Manson's cult of killers, after the
pistol she trained on President Gerald Ford didn't go off.

I was there when he [Persico] got shot. . . . They pulled
up alongside. . . . They didn't have no balls. . . . They
didn't finish the job. . . . They shot through the car. . . .
Through the door, through the motor. [Persico] got hit
in the mouth. . . . He spit the bullet out. . . .
—Hugh "Apples" MacIntosh, enforcer with the Gallo brothers (no relation to the
vintners) and later with the Profaci crime family, discussing the unsuccessful hit on
Carmine "The Snake" Persico.

curiosity

I've always kinda wondered what it would be like to kill
somebody. . . . I just wanted to see someone die.
—Oliver Terpening, Jr., 16-year-old who shot his 14-year-old friend. When the victim's
three sisters showed up, he shot them, too.

(tales from the) dark side

I hereby befile [sic] the living God and serve only the Dark One, Dracula; to serve him faithfully so I may become one of his faithful servants.
—Arthur Richard Bagg, South African man who stabbed his lover to death, from a note found in a secret space in his bedroom.

I feel like I've got the devil in me and it's got to come out.
—David Emmeloth, Illinois murderer who died in a shoot-out with the police, speaking to his mother before he shot and killed two men in 1978.

You wasn't a cannibal. It's the force of the devil, something forced on us that we can't change.
—Henry Lee Lucas, mass murderer, speaking to his partner in many of his 90 killings, Ottis Toole, in a conversation wire-tapped by the police. Toole was known to have eaten some of the victims.

You will find the little boy by a wooden cross near Tongue Pond. I didn't want to do it. Satan ordered me to. I hope you will kill me, cops, because I don't know why I killed the children.
—William Sarmento, arrested in the murders of two boys in Providence, Rhode Island, in a note sent anonymously to the police.

I renounce God, I renounce Christ. I will serve only Satan. . . . Hail Satan.
—Sean Sellers, who killed three people, including his mother, and became the youngest inmate awaiting execution in Oklahoma. He wrote the above oath in his own blood.

Yes I did it! But it was the devil who told me to do it!. . . . He came to me while I was in the kitchen baking bread. He came to me while I was working in the fields. He followed me everywhere.
—Martha Hazel Wise, who poisoned eleven members of her own family because she was fed up with their constant teasing over her infatuation with a younger man.

day jobs

I do not wish it to be said, however, that I 'dismembered' my victims. I did nothing of the sort. I 'dissected' them in a decent and proper manner. I am not a bungler.
—Charles Avinain, a.k.a. "Charles Avignon," 19th-century French murderer responsible for at least 20 butchered bodies found floating in the Seine River during 1867. By day he worked as a butcher.

Alphonse Capone
Second Hand Furniture Dealer
2220 South Wabash Avenue
—Al Capone's business card.

Between you and me, all I do is grow tomatoes.
—Carmine Galante, a.k.a. "Mr. Lilo," mobster in the Bonnano crime family.

It got so I couldn't get the sight [of dead bodies] out of my mind. Ever since, I'd get blue flashes when I'd been drinking, and would have to kill.
—Harry W. Gordon, morgue janitor turned murderer.

Waxey Gordon is dead. From now on it's Irving Wexler, salesman.
—Waxey Gordon, major Prohibition-era bootlegger who was jailed on income tax evasion charges. Having lost everything, he proclaimed a new identity for himself upon his release from jail. He went into narcotics trafficking instead.

I am a dress contractor.
—Tony Lucchese, Mafioso, when asked to describe his occupation during a Senate hearing.

dear diary

Killed a young girl. It was fine and hot.
—Frederick Baker, British man who murdered an eight-year-old girl in August of 1867, from a page in his diary.

. . . enormous new capacity for self love . . . a whole new confidence and style, an intellectual and moral integrity . . . the real self.
—William Bradford Bishop, Jr., writing about himself in his diary before beating his wife and three children to death and setting them on fire.

I have decided that I think I should become a homo-sexual murderer and shall get hold of young boys . . . and I shall rape them and kill them. . . . My first few victims shall each be killed in a different way, which shall be as follows: Victim No. 1: strangled by hands. . . .
—Ronald Frank Cooper, murderer, writing in his diary.

Soon the satisfaction of looking at corpses probably will pass away and then I will kill! Oh, why was I born?
—Daniel Paul Harrison, murderer of five people, writing in his diary.

We discussed our plans for murdering mother and made them a little clearer. I want it to appear either a natural or an accidental death.
—Pauline Parker, 16-year-old New Zealand girl who plotted her mother's death so she herself could be alone with her 15-year-old girlfriend, Juliet Hume, writing in her diary.

death

Death means peace to me. . . . I'm in hell right now.
—Paula Cooper, 15-year-old who stabbed to death a 78-year-old Bible teacher.

debt collection

I could grab this guy and crush him like grapes.
—Pietro Alfano, Mafia narcotics trafficker and pizza maker, exclaiming how he would extract justice for late payment by a "customer."

decisions

. . . I knew I was either going to kill that girl or myself, and then I decided she was going to be the one to go.
—Willie Grady Cochran, ex-convict who raped and killed a fifteen-year-old girl while on parole in 1955.

delusions of grandeur

What do you think of me now. Am I not Lord Wellington now?
—John Ashton, British robber, at his own hanging. When the trap door opened Ashton managed to scramble back up and shout, "Look at me! I am Lord Wellington!" Ashton was referring to Arthur Wellesly, Duke of Wellington, the British general who defeated Napoleon at the Battle of Waterloo.

If I hadn't gotten busted I'd be sittin' in that chair today.
—Giacomo "Fat Jack" DiNorscio, a mobster who acted as his own counsel at his drug trafficking trial, while pointing to the judge's bench.

I'll never be taken alive.
—Helen Spence Eaton, a.k.a. the "Toughest Woman in Arkansas," in a note found in her prison locker after she escaped from a work camp. Eaton died in a shoot out with police.

It is for me, gentlemen, to pass [judgment] upon you, and not you upon me.
—Richard Lawrence, a house painter who became the first person to attempt the assassination of an American president when he tried to kill President Andrew Jackson, speaking to the jury at his trial.

What did their lives mean in comparison to hundreds of sick and disease-twisted bodies? Just laboratory guinea pigs found on any public street. No one missed them when I failed. My last case was successful. I know now the feeling of Pasteur, Thoreau, and other pioneers.
—"The Mad Butcher of Kingsbury Run," unknown mass murderer who killed and then dismembered at least eleven people in and around the area known as Kingsbury Run in Cleveland, Ohio, in a note mailed to the *Cleveland Press* in 1939.

I lived their lives. I actually was Voltaire. I was the great fighter of the French revolution, Danton. A thousand times, I myself, in my black room saved France singlehanded. I became emotionally involved with these statesmen. . . .
 Sukarno, Indonesian strongman leader, on his early studies

In this truck is a man whose latent genius, if unleashed, would rock the nation, whose dynamic energy would overpower those around him. Better let him sleep?
—Peter William Sutcliffe, a.k.a. "The Yorkshire Ripper," British serial killer, from a note found in his truck.

democracy

Let's vote.

—Butch Cassidy, a.k.a. Robert LeRoy Parker, legendary Old West outlaw who, along with the Sundance Kid, robbed banks and stagecoaches, asking his fellow outlaws whether or not they should kill the guard who refused to open the safe in the mail car of a train in Colorado in 1887. They were holding a gun to the guard's head at the time.

denial

Kidnapping? The only kidnapping I know anything about is Robert Louis Stevenson's.

—Gary Steven Krist, burglar and thief who kidnapped a Florida woman and collected $500,000 in ransom from her family, speaking at his sentencing.

I done a lot of things in my life but I never had nothin' to do with makin' money outa whores.

—Charles "Lucky" Luciano, mobster-founder of the national crime syndicate, who was found guilty of dozens of prostitution-related crimes.

. . . never for one moment did I feel that I had committed an injustice or crime.

—Walther Schultze, national leader of the Association of University Lecturers in Nazi Germany, at a trial for complicity in the killing of 380 people.

I'm no psycho! I have a good mind!

—Howard Unruh, army sharpshooter who shot 13 people to death in a 12-minute rampage in Camden, New Jersey, in 1949.

descriptions

[She] looked like an angel choked with sauerkraut.

—Marie Alexander Becker, who poisoned clients in her dress shop in order to steal their money, describing one of her victims.

He liked guns.

—Meyer Lansky, underworld financial whiz and a founder of the national crime syndicate, on fellow mobster Bugsy Siegel, who was renowned for his violent temper.

Poor dumb cop.

—Lee Harvey Oswald, who assassinated President John F. Kennedy on November 22, 1963, talking to himself after shooting and killing a policeman later that day.

He was a nice gentleman. I thought so right up to the time I cut his throat.
—Perry Smith, escaped convict who killed a farmer and his family, from his confession in 1965.

I just started shooting. That's it. I just did it for the fun of it.
—Brenda Spencer, a 16-year-old high school student in San Diego, explaining why she opened fire with a .22 caliber automatic rifle at an elementary school in 1979, killing two children and injuring several more.

Valachi: Buster looked like a college boy, a little over 6 feet, light complexion, weighed 200 pounds. He also would carry a violin case.

Question: What did he carry in the violin case?

Valachi: A machine gun.

Question: He was quite different from the fellows you were working with at the time?

Valachi: Yes. He looked collegiate like.

—Joseph Valachi, a henchman in the Genovese crime family, talking about an associate "hood," during Senate sub-committee hearings in 1963.

[Klaus] Barbie is known at headquarters as an SS leader who knows what he wants and is enthusiastic. . . . Barbie is dependable in both his ideological approach and character. . . .
—Sturmbannführer Wanninger, high-ranking Nazi, in his report recommending Barbie for promotion to the rank of captain.

desires

If only that S.O.B. is croaked tonight, how happy I will be, how lovely it will be.
—Charles Becker, corrupt New York City police lieutenant, on the impending execution of a gambler.

I want to risk myself in the world. The thought of having security annoys me.
—May Churchill, a.k.a. "Chicago May," Irish-born bank robber and prostitute, upon ending her marriage to her army officer husband.

I'd like to kill about 1,000 more people. . . . When I kill,
I feel a release.
—Wayne Coleman, murderer, after being sentenced to death in 1973.

I want the chair: that's what I've
always wanted. . . . My lawyer told
me there are a hundred of men waiting to die in the chair. I'm asking
the judge if I can have the first
man's place. He's sitting there sweating right now. I'm not sweating. I'm
ready for it.
—Mack Ray Edwards, Los Angeles construction worker who confessed to killing six children, speaking
to the court at his trial. In 1971, while in his cell on death row at San Quentin, he hanged himself.

I hope I get what I deserve.
—Peter Griffiths, who kidnapped a four-year-old girl from a hospital in Blackburn,
England, and then murdered her, in his confession to the police.

I loved to see death in all its forms and phases, and left
no opportunity unimproved to gratify my taste for such
sights. Could I have had my own way, probably I should
have done more [murder].
—Martha Grinder, a 19th-century Pittsburgh woman who slowly poisoned her neighbor to death.

I wanted to make him thoroughly sick so that he would
give me permission to divorce him. . . . I poisoned him
with arsenic.
—Maria Groesbeek, a South African woman who was hanged for killing her husband
with insect poison.

. . . the argument began over a sexual matter . . . but
there was also the desire to see blood flowing.
—Michel Henriot, French fox breeder who killed his wife in order to collect on her
life insurance policy.

When I came to think over what I had read, when I was
in prison, I thought what pleasure it would give me to
do things of that kind once I got out again.
—Peter Kürten, a.k.a. "The Düsseldorf Vampire," on reading the story of Jack the Ripper
while awaiting his trial for the murders of nine women.

[Hanging would be a] real pleasure and a big relief . . .
the only thanks you or your kind will ever get from me
for your efforts on my behalf is that I wish you all had
one neck and I had my hands on it . . .
—Carl Panzram, misanthropic mass murderer, speaking to the Society for the Abolishment of Capital Punishment when they tried to help him avoid execution.

If I could bring the motherfucker back to life, I'd kill
him again.
—Nick Scarfo, boss of the Bruno/Scarfo crime family, after the killing of Vincent
Falcone, a family associate who had the nerve to call Scarfo "crazy."

dinner anyone?

Well, some of it moos, and some of it don't moo.
—Charles Anselmo, mobster involved in the meat packing industry and associate of Joe Bonnano, when asked whether any of his shipments contained horse meat.

[I wanted to live so] I could completely control a person—a person that I found attractive and keep them with
me as long as possible, even if it meant just keeping a
part of them.
—Jeffrey Dahmer, serial killer and cannibal, who kept body parts of his victims in freezers and cooked them in lobster pots.

I don't like barbecue sauce.
—Henry Lee Lucas, mass murderer to whom police attribute 90 murders, on why he
didn't join his partner in many of the killings, Ottis Toole, in eating the victims.

I put the head into a pot, popped the lid on and lit the
stove. Later I listened to music and had a good drink,
also watching some TV as the head was simmering.
—Dennis Nilsen, Briton who killed 15 young men, before being sentenced to life
in prison.

. . . I threw away the strips of flesh I had left, and I confess I did so reluctantly as I had grown fond of human
flesh, especially that portion around the breast.
—Alfred Packer, robber, murderer, and cannibal, describing how he killed and ate some
of the men he led on a failed gold prospecting expedition in Colorado in 1873.

Remember one time I said I wanted me some ribs? Did that make me a cannibal?
—Ottis Toole, an arsonist and serial killer, speaking to his partner, Henry Lee Lucas, in a telephone conversation taped by the police. Toole was known to have practiced cannibalism. Together, Toole and Lucas are believed to have murdered 108 people.

dinner plans

I'm gonna be eatin' spaghetti at home on Sunday.
—Frank Abbandando, a.k.a. "The Dasher," hit man for Murder, Inc., speaking before his murder trial began. He was found guilty.

I'm going to use the best silver tonight. It's going to be like the Last Supper.
—Priscilla Bradford, wife of a Florida optometrist whose murder she carried out with the help of two of her husband's employees, talking about the celebratory dinner they would have after the killing.

I must have a man for supper!
—Sam Brown, outlaw gunman of the Nevada mining camps in the 1850s, shouting as he rode out of the mountains and into town.

disappointment

Only one dead? I thought I could get more. I must have been slow.
—Udham Singh, a Sikh terrorist, to the police after he shot and killed the ex-governor of Punjab and wounded three others at a London meeting in 1940.

disclaimers

I didn't want to hurt them. I only wanted to kill them.
—David Berkowitz, a.k.a. "The Son of Sam," paranoid killer who shot fourteen people and terrorized New York City between 1975 and 1977.

I'm not the monster I'm made out to be.
—Louis Cirillo, drug trafficker arrested as part of a ring that smuggled $200 million worth of heroin into the U.S.

I mean I wasn't born free of sin but I sure couldn't be all the things that people have said—I got torture chambers in my cellar, I'm a murderer, I'm the head of every shylock ring, of every bookmakin' ring, I press buttons and I have enterprise in London, at the airports I get seven, eight million dollars a year revenue out of there, who are they kiddin'? . . .
—Joe Columbo, boss of the Columbo crime family.

The people who come into my places are gamblers. . . . I'm a business man.
—Frank Costello, Mafia boss who made his reputation as a gambling operator and rum runner, taking exception to being introduced as a gambler.

Don't forget, these women were trying to take me, too.
—Sigmund Engel, hustler who claimed to have married 200 women and conned them out of $6 million, speaking to reporters during his trial.

I have no conscience. My conscience is Adolf Hitler.
—Hermann Goering, commander in chief of the Luftwaffe.

I had no ill-will toward the President. His death was a political necessity. I am a lawyer, theologian, and politician. I am Stalwart of the Stalwarts.
—Charles J. Guiteau, assassin of President James A. Garfield, from his own version of Garfield's obituary.

I didn't do anything in my entire career which I though was criminal.
—Michael Milken, who pleaded guilty to conspiracy, securities fraud, and mail fraud, after his release from prison.

I'm not a greedy person. I gave away more than I kept, that's for sure.
—Nicholas P. Mitola, professional gambler, drug dealer, and associate of the Lucchese crime family, who was convicted of drug charges. He referred to himself as a "walking crime wave" and had committed "literally thousands" of crimes.

Men like myself could not have existed without the victims' covetous, criminal greed.
—Joseph "Yellow Kid" Weil, early-20th-century hustler who claimed to have conned 2,000 people out of more than $3 million.

distinction

I like to kill. It sets a man apart if he can kill.
—Glennon Engleman, murdering Missouri dentist who seduced his female patients and
then had them marry his future victims.

divine direction

I have no regrets. I acted alone and on orders from God.
—Yigal Amir, assassin of Israeli Prime Minister Yitzhak Rabin.

I never had the slightest doubt as to the divinity of
the inspiration. . . .
—Charles Guiteau, speaking about his assassination of President James A.Garfield.

What is pure love? Communism. . . . In other words, Paul
was saying give your body to be burned. Set it afire if
necessary; to convey a revolutionary message, but be
sure you've got Communism in your heart.
—Jim Jones, the reverend and cult leader whose followers committed mass suicide
by drinking poisoned Kool-Aid.

divine intervention

I'm gonna die as I've lived and
you ain't gonna change me in a
few minutes.
—Thomas "Black Jack" Ketchum, outlaw train robber of the Old West, to a priest on his execution day.

Before Christ came into my life, the realities of the ma-
terialistic world had the priority in my daily life.
—Manuel Noriega, Panamanian dictator who was extradited to the United States and
imprisoned on drug-related charges, on being a born-again Christian.

I'm glad I killed him—he was a satyr!
—Violette Noziere, French teenager who poisoned her father in 1934.

I never wanted to kill him. . . . Providence took charge
of the situation.
Henry K. Thaw, a millionaire who, in 1906, shot and killed renowned architect Stanford
White over White's affair with Thaw's wife, Evelyn Nesbitt.

double-talk

We are against terrorism. But what is terrorism?
—Hafez Asad, Syrian president.

Betting is a human frailty, but it isn't evil in itself.
—William L. Dawson, a 1930s and '40s Chicago lawyer and ward committeeman said to be beholden to Al Capone.

I never accused anybody of anything in my life. I never made peace with anybody that fought me.
—George "Bugs" Moran, Chicago mobster.

I'll give up after I'm killed!
—Bob Rogers, American outlaw murderer and train robber, shouting to lawmen who surrounded the house in which he had barricaded himself. He was killed in the subsequent shoot-out.

I have lied in good faith.
—Bernard Tapie, French businessman accused of fixing a soccer game in which the club he owned participated.

drugs

It must have been the LSD.
—Dale Merle Nelson, Canadian whose murder rampage left nine people dead and butchered, to a policeman.

duh!

You would have to be an absolute moron not to know murder was against the law.
—Pauline Parker, 16-year-old New Zealand girl who plotted her mother's death so she herself could be alone with her 15-year-old girlfriend, Juliet Hume.

duty

. . . it will be the sublime task of German women and girls of good blood acting not frivolously but from a profound moral seriousness to become mothers to children of soldiers setting off to battle. . . .
—Heinrich Himmler, Nazi, Reichsführer-SS, head of the Gestapo and Waffen SS, and minister of the interior of Nazi Germany, on the duty of German women during World War II.

I didn't like politics at all. . . . I was the happiest man in all
the world with my psychiatry, poetry, friends and family.
—Radovan Karadzic, Bosnian Serb leader, former psychiatrist, and indicted war criminal.

I wish I didn't have to carry on the Lord's work in such
a conspicuous capacity.
—Sister Aimee Semple McPherson, a revivalist preacher who made millions of dollars, lived lavishly, and was indicted for obstruction of justice after she falsely claimed
she had been kidnapped—a lie apparently concocted to cover a few days she spent
having an affair.

efficiency

Oh, about one minute and 40 seconds flat.
—John Dillinger, infamous bank robber of the 1920s and '30s, when asked how long
it took to rob a bank.

What's the good of knocking a woman about with your
fists? You should hit with a hammer, the same as I did.
—Tony Mancini, a.k.a. "The Brighton Trunk Murderer," small-time British criminal found
not guilty of murder in 1934. In 1976, Mancini confessed that he had killed a woman
and stuffed her body into a trunk.

enthusiasm

Why, that's better than sex!
—Bonnie Brown Heady, alcoholic ex-wife of a bank robber, on her new boyfriend's plan to kidnap the
son of one of the richest men in Kansas City, Missouri.

[I] plunged into Satanism with everything I had.
—Sean Sellers, who killed three people, including his mother, and became the youngest
inmate awaiting execution in Oklahoma.

euphemism

I would be lying if I said I didn't enjoy giving a guy a deal.
—Mickey Cohen, mobster, speaking about murder.

[My father] met with an accident. He was murdered.
—Joe Columbo, boss of the Columbo crime family.

If you don't pay the thousand, I'm not going to shout;
I'm not going to holler. I'm going to hit you in the head.
—William Daddano, a.k.a. "Willie Potatoes," Chicago hit man for Mafia boss Sam
Giancana, to a debtor who wasn't keeping up with his payments. "Hit" means kill.

Today, you see the sun. Tomorrow, Tony, he no see
the sun.
—Stefano Magaddino, godfather of the Buffalo-Niagara Falls crime family, explaining to one of his underlings what would happen to "Tony," a "soldier" who had
cheated him.

Max Rubin: I got homesick.
Louis Lepke: How old are you . . . ?
Rubin: I'm 48.
Lepke: That's a ripe old age.
—Max Rubin, a gangster working for notorious mobster Louis Lepke in the garment
industry, explaining why he was back in New York City when he was supposed
to be working out of town. He had returned to New York against Lepke's wishes.
Days later Rubin was shot, but not killed; he testified against Lepke at Lepke's
murder trial.

Take care of your problem.
—Standard Mafia order to kill.

The guard took sick and died all of
a sudden. He died of heart trouble.
I guess you would call it a punc-
ture of the heart.
—Robert Franklin Stroud, a.k.a. "The Bird Man of Alcatraz," telling another convict how prison guard
Andrew Turner had died. Of course it was Stroud who had killed him.

We're taking off the Santa Claus suit. There are a lot of
guys who are going to start getting hurt.
—Unknown mobster from a wiretapped conversation.

We took Stevie for a ride, a one-way ride.
—Hymie Weiss, O'Bannion gang boss, uttering the phrase he coined, on the
execution of a rival gangster who was invited to take a car ride from which only
Weiss returned.

excellence

I went back to Brooklyn under orders to do the best job
I ever had done—to smash everything in the place and
beat everybody up. I watched my men go inside, and
then I went to a street stand and bought a package of
cigarets [sic]. I heard an awful din and saw people jumping out of the windows and screaming on the fire escapes. I just kept smoking a cigaret [sic] as the people
ran by me, revolver-shots from my men popping out to
keep them on the run. I went to a corner drugstore and
telephoned my employer that everything was O.K. He told
me afterward that it was the best job he ever saw done.
—Dopey Benney, gang boss of the East Side of New York City, in his confession to
the district attorney in 1915.

I'm proud of them. . . . They can do everything. They can
fight, they can shoot, they can kill.
—Igor "X," a Russian gangster and smuggler, on the capabilities of his gang members.

exceptions

Outside of the killings, we have one of the lowest crime
rates in the country.
—Marion Barry, Washington, DC, mayor who was caught on videotape smoking crack.

If I got a thrill, I didn't take anything.
—William Heirens, robber, rapist, arsonist, and murderer.

We don't rob Southerners, especially Confederate soldiers. But Yankees and detectives are not exempt.
—Jesse James, legendary train and bank robber of the Old West, during an Arkansas
train heist.

excuses

In the psychiatrist's opinion, I ex-
perienced a breakdown precipitated
by many factors external to me and
related to the workplace.
—Ellen F. Cooke, who earned $125,000 as treasurer of the National Episcopal Church, on why she stole
$2.2 million from the church and used the money to buy homes, jewelry, and limousine rides.

existential crises

What does bloodshed get you but more bloodshed?
—J. Harvey Bailey, bank robber during the "golden age" of Dillinger, Bonnie and Clyde, and others, on his decision not to fight his recapture in 1933.

The President's death was a sad necessity, but it will unite the Republican party and save the Republic. Life is a fleeting dream, and it matters little when one goes. A human life is of small value. During the war thousands of brave boys went down without a tear. I presume the President was a Christian and that he will be happier in Paradise than here.
—Charles J. Guiteau, assassin of President James A. Garfield, from his own version of Garfield's obituary.

Everything turns gray when I don't have at least one mark on the horizon. Life then seems empty and depressing.
—Victor "The Count" Lustig, con man who once fleeced Al Capone.

Why could not mother die? Dozens of people, thousands of people, are dying every day. So why not mother, and father too?
—Pauline Parker, 16-year-old New Zealand girl who plotted her mother's death so she herself could be alone with her 15-year-old girlfriend, Juliet Hume, writing in her diary.

experience

I was in this business for ten years before you ever walked into a bank with a gun in your hand. You're an upstart.
Edward Wilhelm Bentz, notorious bank robber who left the circus as a teenager to embark upon a life of crime, speaking to equally notorious bank robber John Dillinger, when Dillinger had the nerve to question one of Bentz's schemes.

explanations

Tonight I tried to kill myself but Sonja put herself between my knife and my throat.
—Mohammed Abdullah, a.k.a. Joseph Howk, Jr., writing in his diary about his ex-girlfriend Sonja Hoff, who he shot to death on a Berkeley, California, campus.

I was in a funny mood. She seemed to insist on coming in. I just happened to look around and saw a hammer in the kitchen. On the spur of the moment I hit her. She gave me a shout and that seemed to start me off more and I hit her a few times, I don't know how many.
—Margaret Allen, British transsexual who murdered a homeless woman who had come to her house begging. Allen was hanged.

I was a hungry wolf. I had a large family. I had to hunt or starve. I learned how to hunt. And I kept it up.
—Moe Annenberg, 1920s mobster.

Just to see if I could, and not worry about it afterwards.
—Penny Bjorkland, an 18-year-old, on why she murdered a gardener.

I couldn't stop killing. It got easier each time.
—William Bonin, a.k.a. "The Freeway Strangler."

If you had to deal with an animal like that, Judge, you'd have done the same damn thing.
—Russell A. Bufalino, boss of the Pittstown, Pennsylvania, crime family, explaining to the judge at his extortion trial that it was necessary to "hit" a witness who owed him money.

I don't know. I just got caught up in all the excitement.
—Thomas Crook, teenager who admitted being part of a gang that was charged with first degree murder in the death of 16-year-old Eddie Polec, on why he used a baseball bat.

All we wanted was an all female lab.
—Joyce Lisa Cummings, who beat to death the man in whose optometry lab she worked.

I got angry and I hit her with the gun and it went off.
—Amy Fisher, a.k.a. "The Long Island Lolita," who shot her married lover's wife in the head.

Senator, I'm the best goddamned lay in the world.
—Virginia Hill, mob "bagman" (money carrier) and girlfriend of mobster Bugsy Siegel, when asked by Senator Charles W. Tobey, during Senate hearings, why she was an underworld favorite.

I'm going to shoot some pheasants.
—Sam "Golf Bag" Hunt, hit man for Al Capone and Murder, Inc., who was known for carrying a shotgun in his golf bag, to a police detective who found the gun, along with Hunt's golf clubs, in Hunt's bag.

You cannot make a good plank out of rotten wood so she was better off dead.
—Kuznetsof, Russian criminal who murdered six people, including his daughter, about whom he said the above.

Everybody kept their shoes there. The maids . . . everybody.
—Imelda Marcos, wife of the corrupt de facto dictator of the Philippines, President Ferdinand Marcos, explaining why her closet was found to contain 6,000 pairs of shoes.

I killed these people and I believe I did the right thing. All of them were suffering and all of them were great nuisances. So I got rid of them.
—Frederick Mors, a porter at a home for the elderly, who poisoned 17 of its inhabitants from 1914 to 1915, recounting his reasoning.

I didn't have to pour it on—but I wanted a reputation. I wanted to be known as the smartest, youngest, and toughest hood.
—Morris "Red" Rudensky, a.k.a. Max Motel Friedman, robber, expert safecracker, and escape artist, on why he so fiercely beat up a gangster who wanted a bigger share of a robbery.

I had a bad day.
—Susan Smith, South Carolina mother who confessed to killing her two sons by strapping them into their car seats and rolling the car into a lake, to a police investigator the day after her sons were reported missing.

I just don't like Mondays. . . . I did this because it's a way to cheer up the day. Nobody likes Mondays.
—Brenda Spencer, a 16-year-old high school student in San Diego, explaining why she opened fire with a .22 caliber automatic rifle at an elementary school in 1979, killing two children and injuring several more.

I am burning some trash.
—William Spinelli, California man who murdered his wife and then burned her body, to his son when the boy arrived home and saw smoke rising from the backyard incinerator.

When a person dies his mind leaves him and goes into another body. My mind was from Legs Diamond.
—John Victor Terry, 20-year-old Briton who shot a bank guard to death for no apparent reason. "Legs" Diamond was a notorious gangster.

Why do they pull a black cap over your face and let it remain until you're dead? Because the high voltage of electricity will make your eyes pop out of your head!
—Unknown death row inmate, from a series of interviews compiled by convicted murderer Frank Blazek.

If I don't get dignity, I take it.
—Luis S. Velez, New York City man who shot two police officers who he claimed called him racist names and arrested him.

I want those fucking shoes.
—Michael Vernon, psychiatric patient who had already confessed to killing two taxicab drivers, speaking to the manager of a shoe store after being told his size was out of stock. Vernon then shot eight people, killing five.

He should have gone into the club, clients or no clients, lined everybody up against the wall and rat-a-tat-tat.
—Domenico Violi, Calabrian-born mobster who moved to Parma, Ohio, telling one of his colleagues how a hit should have been carried out.

fairness

I'm a parlay player. I always made it a practice to spend on Mabel what I got from Jane.
—Sigmund Engel, hustler who claimed to have married 200 women and conned them out of $6 million, speaking to reporters during his trial.

fame

The day will come when I will have too much of an identity and then there won't be any place I can go. I ran out of space once they knew who I was, once I made the "big time" and had all the cops and feds after me. The job was over. I was out of work.
—Basil Banghart, a.k.a. "The Owl," robber and four-time prison escapee of the 1930s, who was known for his large head and eyes and served out his life sentence in Alcatraz prison.

They've blamed everything on me but the Chicago fire.
—Al Capone, legendary mobster who controlled Chicago during the 1920s and '30s.

family ties

I saw that mother was looking at me and I had the feeling that it was not permitted for her to look at me in this manner. I therefore took the clothes hanger and struck her over the head . . . she fell over and lost consciousness. . . . Father continued to play the organ and praise Jesus.

—Frank Alexander, teenage satanic cultist who, along with his father, hacked his mother and sister to death.

We've killed my wife and other daughters. It was the hour of killing.

—Harald Alexander, Frank's father.

It takes courage to kill your own daughter.

—Jacques Algarron, urging his wife, Denise Labbe, to kill her two-and-a-half-year-old daughter as a way of demonstrating her love for him. Labbe drowned the girl and she and Algarron were tried for murder; Labbe received a life sentence and Algarron 20 years hard labor.

If you mention this matter again, may the gods curse you with daughters as lecherous as mine; or let your wives turn out that way also.

—Augustus, emperor of Rome, to those expressing sympathy for his banished daughter Julia. Augustus threw Julia out of Rome because she was a "nymphomaniac" and an embarrassment to the family.

I don't dislike [Scotty]. I just want to be able to do whatever I want in my own home, and I don't particularly enjoy keeping doors shut and keeping fully dressed all the time.

—Stephanie Baker, Kentucky woman who strangled her 10-year-old stepson.

I'm not going to stab my sister in the back for nothing.

—Michael Barbieri, indicted-on-drug-charges brother of Paula Barbieri, the woman O.J. Simpson was dating at the time his ex-wife Nicole was slashed to death, to reporters wanting "dirt" on his sister.

If that will kill grandma—then grandma must die.

—Willie Morris Bioff, movie business extortionist, relating how he told a labor representative of the Chicago movie exhibitors that there had to be two operators in each projection booth, even if it meant financial ruin for the exhibitors.

He could have been more self-centered, placing personal tranquility over sacrifice. Instead he chose to help
his family.
—Joe Bonnano, New York City Mafia boss, on his father's choice to join the Mafia
rather than the priesthood.

I'm going to whack that son of a bitch one of these days. I'm getting tired of him screwing up.
—Anthony Caponigro, a.k.a. Tony Bananas, consigliere to Mafia boss Angelo Bruno, on Caponigro's
brother-in-law, Freddy Salerno.

[I] would walk over my grandmother if necessary.
—Charles Colson, Special Counsel to President Richard Nixon, on what he would do
to insure Nixon's re-election.

They say I was brought up in a life of crime. Would you
believe any father would bring up his son to do anything bad?
—Joe Columbo, boss of the Columbo crime family.

I'll have to give him a .45 and put him to work for me.
—Momo Salvatore "Sam" Giancana, Cosa Nostra overlord of the Chicago area, on what
do with his son-in-law.

I think I played an important role from the day we shot
Paul Castellano.
—Sammy Gravano, a.k.a. "The Bull," henchman under Mafia don John Gotti who
admitted killing 19 people, when asked if he played an important role in the
Gotti family.

I am sorry to hear uncle and auntie are dead. I was
their favorite.
—Thomas Ronald Lewis Harries, 24-year-old Englishman who lived with his aunt and
uncle on their farm, speaking to the police after it was determined that Harries had
bludgeoned the couple to death.

I just wondered how it would feel to shoot grandma.
—Edmund Emil Kemper III, a California man who murdered and dismembered eight
people, including his grandparents.

We would kill people that disrespected our family, and I
thought that was good.
—Philip Leonetti, Philadelphia-based Mafia underboss.

I don't care how long it takes, they're both dead.

—Nick Scarfo, boss of the Bruno/Scarfo crime family, regarding his sister and nephew, when he found out that they had turned government witnesses.

I really loved that girl! I'll kill her!
—Charles Howard Schmid, murderer who lured a 15-year-old girl to the desert and killed her.

fate

If they get there, they get there. And if they don't, they don't.
—Joe Tom Meador, American soldier during World War II, talking to a fellow soldier about the fate of the "Quedlinburg Treasure" Meador was ordered to guard, but instead mailed to his parents in Texas.

favors

I didn't invent sex, nobody had to come to my apartment who didn't want to. I was really doing them a favor.
—Pearl "Polly" Adler, 1920s–'40s New York City madam with organized crime connections.

(legitimate) fears

Well, I missed.
—Joseph Alonzo, a.k.a. "Little Joe," drug addict who turned informant after he failed in a murder attempt on mob boss Giacomo DiNorscio. Alzano was responding to the question, "What was it about the shooting of DiNorscio that now leads you to fear for your own life?"

You think it's easy having all these women? I have a lot of worries. What if one of my wives has AIDS? What if she has V.D? I have to trust in God's strength to keep me free of such things.
—David Koresh, Branch Davidian cult leader who, along with his followers, burned to death when their compound caught fire during an ill-fated raid by the FBI and ATF. Koresh took numerous "wives," some as young as 13.

I want to get it off my mind, I can't go to heaven now.
—Wendell Willis Lightbourne, a Bermuda teenager who murdered three women while working as a golf caddy, in his confession to the police.

. . . bullets tipped with garlic. . . .

—John Torrio, a.k.a. "Terrible John," boss of Chicago's South Side mob, as he lay on a sidewalk after being shot, worrying that the bullets had been tipped with garlic and would poison him. Al Capone's hit men rubbed garlic on their bullets, believing that they would be more lethal. Torrio survived the shooting.

fidelity

Charlie wasn't a bad egg. He just made the mistake of running around with other women.

—Nina Housden, Michigan housewife who strangled and then butchered her husband. She was caught with his dismembered, decomposing body in the trunk of her car as she sought a burial site. The above was said to reporters after she was sentenced to life imprisonment in 1948.

the fifth amendment

I have nothing to fear. My record is an open book.

—David Beck, International Brotherhood of Teamsters president convicted of income tax evasion, testifying before a Senate Select Committee on Improper Activities in the Labor or Management Field. Under questioning Beck proceeded to invoke the Fifth Amendment over 200 times.

I take the Fifth on the horse and the broad.

—Fiore "Fifi" Buccieri, personal hit man of Mafia boss Sam Giancana and the Chicago Syndicate, answering questions at a federal probe on mob activity; the questions were about the Playboy centerfold-girlfriend of Buccieri's brother, Frank, and the fact that Frank had given her a horse as a gift.

final words

I'm gonna miss the first night ball game of the season.

—Frank Abbandando, a.k.a. "The Dasher," hit man for Murder, Inc., awaiting execution in the electric chair.

I can't help it, bambino, but I'm going.

—Louis "Two Guns" Alterie, Chicago bootleg-era gangster known for carrying two .38 caliber guns, uttering his last words as he lay on a sidewalk, fatally shot by an unknown gunman, his head in his wife's arms.

Never did see so many ugly people in my life.

—Charles Birger, bootlegger and killer, while gazing out at the people gathered at the gallows for his execution. To his guards he added, "They're no better looking than you fellows."

This is just one more step down the road of life that I've been heading all my life. Let's go.

—Jesse Walter Bishop, ex-paratrooper turned robber and murderer, moments before being put to death in the gas chamber.

I wish to die as I have lived, completely alone.

—Mildred Mary Bolton, housewife who shot her husband six times because she was jealous of the attention he paid his secretary, in her suicide note at the Illinois jail where she was serving a life sentence.

I can't die with my boots on, please pull them off.

—Charles Bryant, a.k.a. "Black Face Charlie," speaking his dying words after being fatally shot by a deputy U.S. marshal in 1891.

Vive l'anarchie!

—Santo Caserio, Italian anarchist who stabbed the president of France to death in 1894, spoken on the guillotine.

I'm going down with my six-guns!

—Joel Collins, train robber, moments before dying in a shoot-out with soldiers in Kansas in 1877.

I'm sorry for your trouble. Tell the mayor that I'm sorry to be causing the city so much trouble.

—Frederick W. Cowan, a.k.a. the "Second Hitler," neo-Nazi who shot and killed five people when he lay siege to an office building on Valentine's Day in 1977, speaking to the police shortly before killing himself.

I killed the President because he was the enemy of the good people—the good working people. I am not sorry for my crime.

—Leon Czolgosz, the 28-year-old laborer who shot and killed President William McKinley in 1901, speaking from his seat in the electric chair.

I dare you to hang me!

—Hannah Dagoe, Irish-born thief sentenced to death in 1673. As she was about to be hanged, she grappled with her executioner and leapt off the platform before the hangman could do the job, an apparent last gesture of defiance.

Don't mind me, boy. I'm done for. Don't surrender! Die game!

—Bob Dalton, member of the train-and-stagecoach-robbing Dalton Brothers, to his brother as he lay dying after a shoot-out with lawmen in 1892.

I've been looking forward to this lot!
—Edgar Edwards, Briton who killed a family of three in an effort to acquire their property for himself, to a chaplain moments before he was hanged in 1903.

. . . let's get on with it.
—Hurbie Franklin Fairris, Jr., who killed a police detective during a robbery, speaking to his executioner moments before dying in the electric chair.

I'd just as soon be fishing.
—Jimmy Glass, convicted of murdering a Louisiana couple in 1987, uttering his last words while being strapped into the electric chair.

I came here to die, not make a speech.
—Crawford Goldsby, a.k.a. "Cherokee Bill," outlaw robber and murderer, when asked if he had anything to say before the noose was put around his neck at his hanging.

Yeah. I'd like you to sit on my lap as they close the door in there.
—John "Jack" Gilbert Graham, who sabotaged the plane flight his mother was on, killing her and 43 others in the process, speaking his last words to a reporter as he was sitting in the death chamber.

I have faced death too many times to be disturbed when it actually comes.
—John Heath, robber and cattle rustler of the Old West. He was sentenced to life in prison but instead was hanged by a group of vigilante miners to whom he said the above.

In the circumstances, you might make that a double!
—Neville Heath, British Air Force veteran who was sentenced to hang after murdering two women, amending his last request, which was for a shot of whiskey.

Every man for his principles. Hurrah for Jeff Davis! Let her rip!
—Boone Helm, outlaw and member of the Old West gang led by "Three-Fingered Jack" Gallagher, as the noose was being placed around Helm's neck at his hanging by vigilantes in 1864.

What harm have I done? Have I put anyone to death?
—Marcus Didius Julianus, a Roman senator who bought the rulership of Rome at an auction in A.D. 193. After a 66-day reign during which he found his leadership scorned, he was overthrown, and asked the above just before he was beheaded.

All for Germany!
—Wilhelm Keitel, general field marshal of the Nazi Army, shouting his last words as he fell through the trap door at his hanging in 1946.

Let her rip!
—Thomas "Black Jack" Ketchum, train robber, speaking his last words to the hangman just before the trap door opened. An incorrectly tied rope caused Ketchum's head to be ripped from his body.

I deserved this fate. It is a debt I have owed for a wild and reckless life. So long everybody!
—William Preston Longley, gunman of the American Old West who was credited with 30 killings, speaking his last words before being hanged.

I'm fit as a fiddle, and ready to hang.
—Kenneth Neu, a would-be nightclub crooner, singing his farewell moments before he was hanged for the murders of two men.

Hurry it up . . . I could hang a dozen men while you're fooling around!
—Carl Panzram, misanthropic mass murderer, speaking to his executioner moments before being hanged.

Tell them in the kitchen to fry Glenn's eggs on both sides—he likes them that way.
—"Iron Irene" Schroeder, bank robber who shot and killed a policeman, giving instructions to the guards about her lover's dining preferences. They were her last words.

French-Canadian bean soup. I want to pay. Let me leave them alone!
—Dutch Schultz, a.k.a. Arthur Flegenheimer, New York mobster, speaking his last words. Schultz ranted nonsense throughout the two days he lay dying from bullet wounds suffered during a mob-ordered hit.

I've been expecting it. The bastards never forget.
—Roger "Terrible" Touhy, Chicago area bootlegger, uttering his dying words after being gunned down in the street. He was killed by Al Capone's gang, still angry years after Touhy had shut them out of his territory.

We're dead. C'mon and get us.
—Harry Young, who with his brother, Jennings, shot and killed five Missouri police officers, calling out to the authorities from inside their hideout. Moments later the brothers committed double suicide.

There is no God. It's all below. . . . See, I no scared of electric chair. . . . Lousy capitalists. . . . Go ahead. Push the button.
—Giuseppe Zangara, Italian-born gunman who some say worked for the Mafia, spoken while sitting in the electric chair. Zangara shot and killed Chicago Mayor Anton J. Cermak, but may have been aiming for President Franklin Roosevelt, who was standing at Cermak's side at the time.

foreign relations

When you talk about a massive invasion, you're obviously exaggerating. It's just that some units are being replaced by others. But they, too, will soon be pulled out. The whole question isn't worth a wooden kopeck.
—Yuri Andropov, then Soviet ambassador to Hungary, on the invasion of Hungary.

The reason why the French are so interested in me is because I wounded their Gaulic pride. I proved to them that they're stupid.
—Klaus Barbie, a.k.a."The Butcher of Lyons," Nazi leader.

The Poles shall be the slaves of the German Reich.
—Hans Frank, Nazi governor general of Poland during World War II.

What happens to the Russians, what happens to the Czechs, is a matter of utter indifference to me. Such good blood of our own kind as there may be among the nations we shall acquire for ourselves, if necessary by taking away the children and bringing them up among us.
—Heinrich Himmler, Nazi, Reichsführer-SS, head of the Gestapo and Waffen-SS, and minister of the interior of Nazi Germany, from a speech to SS leaders.

We don't want war. We hate war. We know what war does.
—Saddam Hussein, president of Iraq, shortly before invading Kuwait.

Any act of mercy is a crime against the German people.
—Wilhelm Keitel, general field marshal and chief of staff of the High Command of the Armed Forces of Nazi Germany, justifying the massacres that took place in Russia.

We will bury you.
—Nikita Khrushchev, U.S.S.R. Communist Party secretary general, on relations with the U.S.

friendship

I have no plans to look him up and I hope he doesn't look me up.
—Joe Adonis, gangster, when asked if he would visit with another deported mobster, Charles "Lucky" Luciano. The two had had a falling out, the consequences of which could be inferred from Adonis' remarks.

Believe me, General, the Soviet people are Hungary's
best friends.
—Yuri Andropov, then ambassador to Hungary and later secretary general of the
U.S.S.R.'s Communist Party, on the Soviet invasion of Hungary.

It makes you wonder. Is this son of a bitch senile, or is
he just a fucking nut? . . . What the fuck. This is a new
kind of plea bargain, or what? Go to the slammer or write
your memoirs and make your friends look lousy? . . . But
that's the remarkable thing about these cock suckers,
Paul. maybe they can't read or write, but they can remember. It's like they have another sense. It's unbelievable.
You know this guy . . . can't read, can't write. But he can
sing you an entire opera, word for word. All the parts.
Fucking soprano shit.
—Joe N. Gallo, consigliere of the Gambino crime family, speaking to his boss, Paul
Castellano, about Mafioso Joseph Bonanno's published autobiography, *A Man of Honor.*

frugality

I never had more than two maids.
—Carolyn Rothstein, wife of Arnold Rothstein, a.k.a. "The Brain," "The Man Uptown,"
and "The Big Fellow," an operator of illegal gambling and loan-sharking operations in
New York City during the 1920s, who was known for living modestly.

frustration

We've been beating him and beating him but he won't
die!
—Priscilla Bradford, wife of a Florida optometrist whose murder she carried out with
the help of two of her husband's employees, asking her mother for advice over the
phone during the murder. Her mother replied, "Just beat him some more until you're
sure he's dead. Then call the police."

. . . the son-of-a-bitch won't die!
—Janice Gould, who, along with her boss's wife and an office mate, helped kill her
optometrist-boss. The above was spoken in the midst of the murder.

I have a lot of friends. Do you know I used to work for
the KGB? I went out on drug raids with them on the
Afghan border. I taught those guys everything they know
. . . and no one is grateful.
—Ted Kasyanov, Russian strongman arrested in Russia for murder and kidnapping.

Can't anybody shoot that guy so he won't bounce back up?
—Dutch Schultz, a.k.a. Arthur Flegenheimer, New York mobster, talking about rival gangster "Legs" Diamond, who survived several assassination attempts.

gifts

Hearty greetings to an old friend.
—Thomas Mathieson Brown, from the card on a cake sent as a gift to his wife's elderly uncle. The cake was laced with strychnine, which made the uncle ill and killed his housekeeper.

goals

I want to master life and death.
—Ted Bundy, serial killer.

. . . we fired to hit.
—Mike Tyson, heavyweight champion boxer convicted of rape, on gun use during his childhood life of crime.

god complexes

I am Jesus Christ. In the name of the omnipotent God, I announce the end of the world. No one, neither the Americans nor the Soviets, will be saved. There will be destruction.
—Mehmet Ali Agca, interrupting his trial for the attempted assassination of Pope John Paul II in 1981.

See, nobody believed that they could shoot at the god.
—Mickey Cohen, mobster, shocked that one famous mobster, Vito Genovese, had the nerve to order a hit on another famous mobster, Frank Costello. Costello survived and apparently forgave Genovese.

Nobody can come in here but Jesus Christ!
—Walter Ferguson, New York City man who murdered his neighbor, to the police when they came to his apartment in order to arrest him.

I am dying like Jesus on the cross . . . without fault.
—Willi Frey, Nazi secret service officer who worked at the Mauthausen concentration camp where 700,000 people were killed during World War II, speaking moments before he was hanged for war crimes.

When we depart, let the earth tremble.
—Joseph Goebbels, Nazi Propaganda Minister.

Let your verdict be, it was the Deity's act, not mine.
—Charles J. Guiteau, assassin of President James A. Garfield, to the jury at his trial in 1881.

If you want aid against me, ask God, not man.
—Edward Hickman, a college student who raised money for his tuition by kidnapping and murdering, from a ransom note.

. . . It's not what I think, it's what I am.
—David Koresh, Branch Davidian cult leader, when asked if he thought he was God.

I would have made a good Pope.
—Richard Nixon, U.S. president who was forced to resign because of the Watergate scandal.

gratitude

Thanks.
—Ruth Ellis, British nightclub manager and model, who shot her race car driver lover to death, upon being told she would be charged with murder.

I have been very well treated at the Lewis and Clark County Jail, and I would like to thank all of the jail staff publicly for their kindness and consideration.
—Theodore Kaczynski, Unabomber suspect, in a letter to the editor printed in the Helena, Montana, *Independent Record*. Kaczynski wrote the letter prior to being moved from Helena to Sacramento, California, where he was formally charged in the Unabomber case.

Well, Master, I suppose this is one more feather in your cap!
—Gertrude Morris, who shot her husband to death because she was jealous of the attention he paid his secretary, to her lawyer, at whom she was mad because she received a relatively light sentence of eight years. She apparently felt she deserved worse, shouting, "I owe society a life!"

greetings

We're here to kill you.
—Felix Alderisio, a.k.a. "Milwaukee Phil," hit man and debt collector for the Chicago mob, upon entering the office of a lawyer who had apparently lost money for the mob. The lawyer began to plead for his life and begged Phil to call his mob boss on the phone. Phil finally agreed, saying, "It's a little irregular, but just to show you there's no hard feelings, I'll do it. If he [Phil's boss] wants to cancel the hit, it's okay with me. I'll get paid anyway." The lawyer's life was spared only after he agreed to pay back $68,000 plus interest.

Well Mister Mad Man, how are you?
—Florence Ferrara, paranoid murderer, greeting Dr. Marion Klinefelter, a bone surgeon, before shooting him in the head as he sat at his desk.

Hello, sucker.
—Maurice Paul Holsinger, crook who specialized in the "matrimonial con," in which he presented himself as an eager, marriage-minded bachelor and then absconded with his victims' savings. He eluded the authorities by disguising himself as a woman when he traveled, and said the above to the police, when, upon his capture at an airport, they pulled off his wig.

What if I was to say I was Jesse James and told you to hand out that tin box of money—what would you say?
—Jesse James, legendary train and bank robber of the Old West, robbing the clerk at a fair grounds in Kansas City, Missouri, in 1872. The cashier replied, "I'd say I'd see you in hell first." James robbed the cashier and many others before he was shot to death in 1882.

Tom McCarty: Excuse me, sir, but I just overheard a plot to rob this bank.
Bank president: Lord! How did you learn of this plot?
McCarty: I planned it. Put up your hands.
—Tom McCarty, member of Butch Cassidy's Wild Bunch outlaws, in a conversation with the president of the First National Bank of Denver, which lost $20,000 in the 1889 heist.

You can come out now. . . . I'm through.
—Hutchie T. Moore, an ex-Chicago policeman who shot and killed the judge and his wife's attorney during his and his wife's divorce settlement proceedings, to officials after his shooting spree was over.

These are our credentials.
—Harry Pierpont, bank robbing cohort of John Dillinger, responding to the sheriff at a Lima, Ohio, prison when asked what his credentials were. Pierpont, who was pretending to be a corrections officer, stated the above as he pulled out a gun. He was in Lima to free John Dillinger from prison.

Kennedy, you son of a bitch.
—Sirhan Bishara Sirhan, Palestinian assassin of Senator Robert F. Kennedy, speaking as he pulled the trigger of his pistol.

gross anatomy

I'd heard that stabbing someone in the kidney would kill him, but I didn't know, so I went ahead and cut his throat, too.

—Billy Lee Chadd, drifter and ex-marine, on how he killed his second murder victim.

It would be longer, but I only count the pieces of white men.

—Annie Christmas, gargantuan stevedore and madam on a floating brothel of the waterways of 19th-century Louisiana, talking about a necklace she made out of the body parts of men who challenged her authority over the swamps.

The anger in my own heart showed me the way to his.

—Charlotte Corday, a.k.a. Marie-Anne Charlotte Corday D'Armans, anti revolutionist who murdered French revolutionary Jean-Paul Marat by stabbing him in the heart.

Show me your heart.

—David Fayson, murderer, speaking to the 13-year-old girl working for him as a prostitute. He then shot her to death—in the chest.

With this arm you will no longer be able to kill Toto Riina!

—Giuseppe "Pino" Greco, bloodthirsty Mafioso whose passion was the supervision of executions, to the son of another Mafioso as he cut off his arm just before killing him.

It was like chopping a small tree. His whole head came off. The rest of him took a few steps, spouting blood like a fountain. Then it sagged down as the head rolled along the deck.

—Albert E. Hicks, 19th-century pirate, describing a murder he committed.

I send you half the kidne[y] I took from one woman . . . the other piece I fried and ate.

—Jack the Ripper, writing in a note attached to a piece of human kidney. The note was signed "From Hell." (No note from Jack the Ripper can be absolutely certified authentic.)

Think of that. With this bum you gotta be a doctor or he floats!

—Harry Strauss, a.k.a. "Pittsburgh Phil," a hit man for Murder, Inc., on a murder victim who didn't sink when his body was thrown into a lake. Gas built up in the intestines of the corpse had caused it to float.

happy holidays

It was in the Christmas spirit. It makes me happy.
—David Bullock, a street hustler who killed a man because he was "messing with the Christmas tree."

hate

I have hated only one person in my life and I have proved the strength of my hatred.
—Charlotte Corday, a.k.a. Marie-Anne Charlotte Corday D'Armans, anti-revolutionist who murdered French revolutionary Jean-Paul Marat, speaking in prison while awaiting execution.

honesty

Well, I didn't inherit any money, Senator.
—Moe Dalitz, renowned bootlegger, during Senate hearings on organized crime, when asked by Senator Estes Kefauver, " . . . you did get yourself a pretty good little nest egg out of rum running, didn't you?"

Goin' to rob a bank.
—"Pretty Boy" Floyd, bank robber, when asked where he was going by a farmer who happened to be sitting in a chair on the street in Sallisaw, Oklahoma. Floyd was on his way to rob Sallisaw Bank. The farmer then responded, "Give 'em hell, Chock!" (Chock was Floyd's nickname.) Floyd made off with $2,530.

I'd just as soon shoot you as look at you.
—John Wayne Gacy, Jr., serial killer who sexually abused his 34 victims before murdering them, to one of his victims.

Look, if I had more bullets, I would have shot 'em all again and again. . . . I was gonna gouge one of the guys' eyes out with my keys afterwards.
—Bernhard H. Goetz, an electrical engineering consultant known as "The Subway Vigilante" and a hero to some, in a statement to police. In 1984, with his unlicensed gun, he shot three of four men he claimed were going to rob him in a New York City subway, paralyzing one.

I've killed three women, and I'd probably do it again unless they get me out of the way.
—Harry W. Gordon, a morgue janitor turned murderer.

I haven't any feelings towards the victims.
—Myron Lance, who, along with his lover, Walter Kelbach, killed six people in December of 1966.

I could kill everyone without blinking an eye.
—Charles Manson, swastika-tattooed mass murderer who created "Helter Skelter," a racist Armageddon.

hope

Ain't losing your nerve, are you, Joe?
—Tom Horn, a former lawman turned hired gun who was convicted of killing a 14-year-old Wyoming boy, speaking to his hangman moments before his death.

humiliation

To kill is one thing, but to be a sneak thief!
—Robert Irwin, who killed two women, after being caught with some petty items from their apartment, to the police during questioning.

humility

After 50 years of so many honors, maybe a little mortification will do me good.
—Giulio Andreotti, former Italian prime minister, charged with colluding with the Mafia.

Does anyone dare teach me?
—Gaius Caesar Caligula, first-century Roman emperor.

I've never made a mistake in my life.
—Raymond Leslie Morris, who kidnapped and sexually assaulted a seven-year-old girl before murdering her in Walsall, England, bragging to his wife.

humor

It just occurred to me that I have only to nod my head once and your throats will be cut straight-away.
—Gaius Caesar Caligula, first-century Roman emperor, when asked what he was laughing about during a banquet.

That's the way I rode through the park, piled back in a limousine, with my foot on a man's neck. We passed two or three cars, and I thought wouldn't it be a joke if they knew.
—Cecelia Cooney, a.k.a. the "Bobbed-Haired Bandit," describing how she terrorized the driver of the limousine she and her husband hijacked during one of their crime sprees.

Hey, you guys, let's go have lunch at Sparks. Whaddaya say? I hear they got great steaks at Sparks.

—Peter Gotti, older brother of Mafia boss John Gotti, speaking to reporters covering John Gotti's trial. Paul Castellano, John Gotti's predecessor as head of the Gambino crime family, was shot to death outside of Sparks Steakhouse by unknown gunmen—one of whom is believed to have been John Gotti.

Shake hands, say goodbye to your old buddy!

—Hans Graewe, a.k.a. "The Surgeon," hit man for a Cleveland, Ohio, gang who was known for his expertise at cutting up bodies. Graewe was talking to his boss, Carmen Zagaria, when he grabbed Zagaria's arm and pushed it into a bucket filled with the head and hands of a colleague whom Graewe had killed and cut into pieces.

I ain't smilin' on either side of me face!

—"Happy" Jack Mulraney, member of the criminal Gophers Gang of New York from the 1890s through the 1910s, addressing the body of the man he had just killed. The man had asked Mulraney why it was that he smiled only on one side of his face. Mulraney's face had been partially paralyzed when he was injured in a street fight as a child.

We have a new disease in town. It's called Chicago amnesia.

—Charles Dion O'Bannion, Chicago North Side mob boss, on the intimidation of witnesses.

Yeah, it was Ladies Night.

—Abe Reles, a paid killer for Murder, Inc., describing how it was that a woman lit the match that set the car that contained the body of much hated mobster Louis "Pretty" Amberg on fire.

We line 'em up facing the wall, but this guy Marameneza [sic] is the only one we want, so we blast him and get out of the joint . . . [outside] I still had the biscuit in my pocket. . . . I edge into that crowd and get up next to a guy who isn't looking and ease that biscuit gently into his pocket and get away. . . . I nearly die laughing when I think of when that guy put his hand in his pocket and found that gun.

—Bo Weinberg, underling to mob boss Dutch Schultz, bragging to his girlfriend about killing Salvatore Maranzano, another mobster, who Weinberg called "Maramaneza."

hypocrisy

[Wife-beaters] should get 10 to 15 years in prison any time [they] beat someone.

—James Brown, a.k.a. the "Godfather of Soul," in an interview. The singer was arrested less than three weeks later for criminal domestic violence.

I'll not have the names of any gangsters mentioned during my trial.
—Sam DeStefano, Chicago Outfit hit man and renowned sadist, to a judge. DeStefano considered himself above other gangsters.

Death would have been better. . . . Sooner or later they're going to get me.
—Raymond Ferritto, a professional burglar who planted the bomb that killed Danny Greene, a Cleveland, Ohio, mobster, speaking about the witness protection program he was in.

identification

You'll know all mine by the tape around their necks.
—Amelia Elizabeth Dyer, a.k.a. the "Reading Baby Farmer," a British woman who boarded and adopted children, telling the police how to identify the bodies of the children she murdered and then dumped in the Thames River.

ignorance

I never heard of it!
—Rose Glyba, a member of a Hungarian murder ring in which women were poisoning their husbands to death, when asked by the judge at her murder trial if she knew of the commandment "Thou shalt not kill."

imagination

Can't you just see those shotgun shells going off in the plane every which way? Can't you just imagine the pilots and the passengers and Mother jumping around?
—John "Jack" Gilbert Graham, who sabotaged the plane flight his mother was on, killing her and 43 others in the process.

impatience

Well, are you going to do it or not?
—Clestell Gay, speaking to her friend Joyce Turner after listening to Turner say she was going to kill her husband some day. Turner then took Gay's .22 caliber pistol, went home, and shot her husband to death.

inconveniences

Hurry it up—I have my linen to do!
—Lydia Adler, housewife convicted of manslaughter in 1/44 and sentenced to be branded on her hand, speaking to the wardens heating up the branding iron.

I don't need this aggravation.
—Tommy Agro, "soldier" (i.e. bodyguard, hit man) for the Gambino crime family, being
questioned by an FBI agent.

indifference

I see Mr. Hoover first, I kill him first. Make no difference,
presidents just the same bunch—all same.
—Giuseppe Zangara, Italian-born gunman who some say worked for the Mafia, who
shot and killed Chicago Mayor Anton J. Cermak. He was apparently trying to shoot
President Franklin Roosevelt, who was standing next to Cermak at the time of the shooting, although Zangara apparently wouldn't have minded killing Roosevelt's predecessor,
President Herbert Hoover, either.

instruction

Smack him in the brains.
—Pietro Alfano, Mafia narcotics trafficker and pizza maker, telling one of his colleagues to carry out a "hit".

This evening at six o'clock you're to be in the cellar with
the rest of the officers. There'll be a rope and you're
going to hang yourself.
—Klaus Barbie, a.k.a. "The Butcher of Lyons," Nazi leader, recounting how he punished
an officer. The officer obliged Barbie's wishes, and once the noose was around his neck,
Barbie kicked away the chair on which the officer was standing.

Kill some of the sons-of-bitches before you die, Charlie!
—William Bonney, a.k.a. "Billy the Kid," legendary outlaw of the Old West, pushing
his mortally wounded friend, Charlie Bowdre, out of their hiding place and toward a
posse of lawmen.

I want you to kill every cop in Akron! You got that? Every cop in the city. Now, right now!
—Rosario Borgio, the Akron, Ohio, Mafia don who couldn't corrupt the Akron police
and so ordered his henchmen to kill them.

I want you to start crying when the cops get here. I want
real tears!
—Priscilla Bradford, wife of a Florida optometrist whose murder she carried out with the
help of two of her husband's employees, speaking to her daughter just after the murder.

Strike so he may feel he is dying.
—Gaius Caesar Caligula, first-century Roman emperor best known for his orgies and
capricious execution orders.

You'll see a guy down near the end of the line that's got to go so bad that he's bent over with his nuts in his hand. You just cut through the line behind him, excuse yourself, and take his money as you pass.
—"Crying Phil," unidentified professional pickpocket, on pickpocketing at the Orange Bowl during a football game.

See how easy it is to kill someone? All you have to do is pull the trigger!
—Patricia Columbo, 19-year-old woman who eventually brutally murdered her parents and younger brother, speaking to two men she tried to persuade to kill her parents. She was aiming a gun at the men at the time.

Before Joey got me to sell my body, he showed me how to exhibit myself to his friends.
—Amy Fisher, a.k.a. "The Long Island Lolita," who shot the wife of her married boyfriend, Joey Buttafuoco. Fisher claims Buttafuoco persuaded her to try prostitution.

If you don't hear nothin,' don't do nothin.' If you hear shots, kill anyone who runs out the front door.
—Anthony Gaggi, Gambino crime family "capo" (captain), to his nephew henchman Dominick Montiglio, on guarding a mob meeting for Paul Castellano's 'coronation' as boss.

Jim Jones: Remove the enemy's life and then your own. But they may try to set up the melee, to be black against black, us against the black Guyanese soldier, and that fight would dishonor Socialism. Then it's best just to lay down our lives . . . and what's that called, congregation?

Response: Revolutionary suicide.
—Jim Jones, the reverend and cult leader whose followers committed mass suicide by drinking poisoned Kool-Aid, in a conversation with his congregation.

Okay, John. Good Night. Get a good night's sleep. And don't bug anyone without my permission.
—Richard Nixon, U.S. president who was forced to resign because of the Watergate scandal, to John Mitchell, his former attorney general and campaign manager.

Leave a couple of fucking heads hanging on a fucking
pole. The stool pigeons that are flaunting it in our face,
they'll think twice . . . before going over to the law.
—Mike Scandifia, mobster in the Gambino Mafia family, referring to a federal wiretapping campaign against the Mafia.

Just keep them for the funeral, although I might give this
one a week's extension.
—Mary Elizabeth Wilson, who was eventually sentenced to death for poisoning her three
husbands, speaking at the wedding reception of her third marriage. She was responding to being asked what to do with the leftover sandwiches and cakes.

intentions

I only hoped to weaken her a little so that she would
agree to a divorce or separation.
—Louis de Deurwaerder, a Belgian man, speaking of the various poisons he gave his
wife, the last of which, a soap and sublimate of mercury enema, killed her.

How can you do a good job when you use an insect
like that?
—Kim Jae-Kyu, head of the Korean Central Intelligence Agency speaking to the president of South Korea, Park Chung-Hee, just before shooting him to death. Kim was referring to the president's bodyguard, Cha Ji-Chul, whom the president favored over
Kim and of whom Kim was jealous.

I intend to kill my wife after I
pick her up from work. I don't want
her to have to face the embarrassment my actions will surely cause her.
—Charles Whitman, who shot 46 people from a bell tower at the University of Texas, in a note.

jealousy

He was a kid. It was all there in front of him. . . . His
whole life . . . sex, fun, all of it! Why should he have it
when I never did? I took it all away from him. . . .
—Stephen Nash, California drifter turned murderer, on a 10-year-old murder victim.

It's in my blood. . . . I love it, being able to be someone else, anyone I please.
—Ferdinand Waldo Demara, Jr., a.k.a. the "Great Impostor," a naval deserter with no professional qualifications, who went on to work as a professor at three universities, as a surgeon, and as a penologist.

I knew I would be set for life.
—George Fresolone, member of the Bruno/Scarfo crime family, on his feelings when he became a "family" member.

Ah . . . this has been a great day! How my knife lapped up their blood!
—Manuel Garcia, a.k.a. "Three-Fingered Jack," Old West bandit, after slashing the throats of some Chinese miners.

judgment

I thought the best thing to do was kill them all.
—Oliver Terpening, Jr., a 16-year-old who shot his 14-year-old friend because he wanted to know what it would be like to watch someone die. When the victim's three sisters showed up, he shot them, too.

justice

It's all over with. . . . It serves me right.
—Johann Hoch, Chicago man who married as many as three times per year, then poisoned his wives and took their money, speaking to the court after he was convicted of murder.

Even though this court may pronounce me guilty a thousand times, the higher court of our great Aryan warrior god pronounces me innocent. Heil Hitler!
—Frank Spisak, Jr., a.k.a. "Frankie Ann Spisak," a Cleveland, Ohio, man and sometime transvestite who shot three people to death, addressing the court before receiving the death sentence. When not dressed in drag Spisak, who idolized Adolf Hitler, wore a short, brush-style moustache.

(small) kindnesses

Sabine, dear, we wanted you to know at once that Frank and I have just finished killing your mother and your sisters.

—Harald Alexander, satanic cultist, who, with the help of his son Frank, hacked his daughter and wife to death. Father and son were sent to an insane asylum.

Because I didn't want to send a man to hell on an empty stomach.

—Robert A. Allison, Confederate Army soldier, cowboy and murderer of an estimated 15 men, when asked why he would eat dinner with an enemy.

While I will not pretend to be Prince Charming, I do think it's fair to say that for two and one-half years now I have done everything to keep your name out of the news and avoid embarrassment for you.

—Ted Bundy, serial killer, to his girlfriend, when she realized what he had been doing in his free time.

Death (other than your own) is no excuse. If the funeral can be held in the late afternoon, we will be glad to let you off for one hour, provided that your share of the work is ahead.

—John Cammillieri, a Mafia henchman hired to speed up work at a construction site, in a message to workers regarding time missed in the event of a death.

From Al.

—Al Capone, a.k.a. "Scarface." The words were printed on the floral wreath sent by Capone to the funeral of a rival gangster, Charles O'Bannion, who Capone had ordered killed.

If the president of the United States, if he's smart, if he needs help, he'd come. I could do a favor for the president . . . .

—Paul Castellano, a.k.a. "Big Paul," Mafia boss in the Gambino family, boasting to his mistress.

I felt I owed it to myself to take control of my own destiny. . . . They've said to me "We're gonna take your life," I say back to them, "Come on, do it." It's my decision.

—Frank J. Coppola, a Virginia murderer sentenced to death, who wanted to speed the process in order to save his teenage sons from embarrassment when they resumed school in the autumn of 1982.

John Dillinger: Is that your money or the bank's?
Farmer: Mine.
Dillinger: Keep it, we only want the bank's.
—John Dillinger, infamous bank robber of the 1920s and '30s, during a bank heist, speaking to a farmer holding $50. Dillinger and his gang took $75,346 of the bank's money.

. . . he grabbed his head, pulled him forward and bit off his earlobe. Bit it off and spat it out! And then he took the guy into his car and drove him to the emergency hospital. About five minutes later they came rushing back to look for that piece of earlobe so they could sew it back on. That was Nicky Valvano.

—Herbie Gross, front man and hotel owner for the Mafia turned federal witness, recounting what mobster Nicky Valvano did to Jimmy "The Brush" Fife.

If I kiss her, I would have to kill her first.
—Edmund Emil Kemper III, a California man who murdered eight people, when asked why he didn't kiss the grade school teacher on whom he had a crush when he was a child.

I was sorry for the wretched woman and so I gave her a bottle of the poison and told her that if nothing else helped her marriage to try that.
—Juliane Lipka, a Hungarian woman who poisoned seven people to death, including her husband, brother, and sister-in-law, speaking about her next-door neighbor, who she also poisoned.

Besides, I always figured that someday I was gonna wind up on a slab and I didn't want to leave a widow and kids cryin' over me.
—Charles "Lucky" Luciano, mobster-founder of the national crime syndicate, who was found guilty of dozens of prostitution-related crimes, on why he patronized brothels.

. . . to put them out of their misery, and, besides, they really are a nuisance to everyone
—Frederick Mors, a porter at a home for the elderly, who poisoned seventeen of its inhabitants from 1914 to 1915.

Go easy. The guy's a sickie and we've made a fortune off him. Give him an easy payment schedule. Whatever we get from him, even if it's ten bucks a week, will be gravy.
—Frank "Funzi" Tieri, New York City-based crime boss, on how to treat a "client" of his loan shark operation.

Most of the people were old enough to die, anyway, or else had some disease that might cause death. I never killed children. I love them.
—Jane Toppan, Massachusetts nurse who confessed to killing 31 people, speaking to the authorities.

Alonzo always told me that he wanted to die in bed. . . . I simply arranged for it.
—Joyce Turner, South Carolina woman who had boasted that she would one day kill her husband Alonzo, speaking to reporters after the trial at which she was sentenced to life in prison.

To my wife, I would like to say happy Mother's Day.
—Joseph Waldholtz, ex-husband of Republican Congresswoman Enid Waldholtz of Utah, after pleading not guilty on charges of financing her campaign using bank fraud and check-kiting. He later pleaded guilty to the charges in a plea-bargain agreement.

labor relations

We hired you as you are and to have anything removed would certainly make you less than we bargained for. Anyone having an operation will be fired immediately.
—John Cammillieri, a Mafia henchman hired to speed up work at a construction site, in a message to workers regarding sick leave.

[The death of a worker] will be accepted as an excuse. But we would like two weeks notice, as we feel it is your duty to teach someone else your job.
—John Cammillieri, a Mafia henchman hired to speed up work at a construction site, in a message to workers regarding sick leave.

What shall I do? I shall never get another position.
—François Benjamin Courvoisier, Swiss valet who killed and robbed his boss in 1840.

I'm already a millionaire from my other businesses, whatever they may be. . . . Anybody who doesn't want to do this and wants to be a wise guy—if they have the courage, they can come with me.
—Giacomo "Fat Jack" DiNorscio, mobster, offering mob membership to the stunned employees of a legitimate business of which he took control.

Can you beat this, they're telling me I'm too tough for the job. Can you imagine what our thing [the Cosa Nostra] is coming to?
—John Gotti, boss of the Gambino crime family, speaking to another Mafia member about Gotti's prospects for the family's top position.

. . . to be perfectly frank, if I had a choice of having a tough ex-convict or a man without a criminal record I am more inclined to take the ex-con. Know why? Because if he is in a boss job he'll keep the men in line and get the maximum work out of them.
—William J. McCormack, a leader of the New York Shipping Association, who was believed to be involved with organized crime.

How would your wife look in black?
—Frank "The Enforcer" Nitti, a henchman for Al Capone, informing a union leader of the possible consequences if the Capone gang wasn't allowed to put one of its own men in the union leadership.

They are just the same as employers in the shop. They see a man is very good and they give him a good job.
—Abe Reles, a paid killer for Murder, Inc., on his bosses.

If this strike is called, I will have you killed. You will be a dead man. You can tell that to the police.
—Samuel Rosoff, henchman for Joseph Fay, the notorious head of the Operating Engineers Union, who employed gangsters for strong-arm work.

Think of what we have here as a business, not a gang.
—David Thai, Vietnamese gang leader, to new recruits for his robbing and shakedown operations.

laments

I have no quarrel with society. It ought to have none with me. I only want what's coming to me. I've been wrong all my life. But I ain't bad. Now, in this hole, I fight the atmosphere, the silence, the bodies. No one feels the hard misery inside me. . . .
—Joseph Paul "Dutch" Cretzer, a bank robber who considered himself more learned than the general prison population, thus the above letter to his wife.

Tougher and tougher things have been getting lately. It's still easy to steal, but it's the fixing that's tougher.
—"Crying Phil," unidentified professional pickpocket, lamenting the fact that he was having to rely more on pickpocketing and less on gambling operations.

Yes, I have always been unhappy, no one has ever tried to understand me. I will always be misunderstood—abnormal, as I have been called—and for all that I am good, with a very warm heart.
—Henri Girard, to his prison guards after being arrested for the poisoning deaths of two people in France.

Fuckin', I tell you what a fuckin' heartbreak. You know you feel like you're being raped with these fuckin' tapes.
—John Gotti, boss of the Gambino crime family, talking to his underling Sammy "The Bull" Gravanno, about how it feels to have had their conversations wiretapped.

Our Mafiya have no culture. They are simply uncultured, stupid people; you cannot reason with them. . . . They lost the most important thing—the respect of the people.
—Ted Kasyanov, Russian strongman arrested in Russia for murder and kidnapping.

I have done my best to get along in your world and now you want to kill me. I say to myself "Ha, I'm already dead, have been all my life. . . . I don't care anything about any of you. . . ."
—Charles Manson, swastika-tattooed mass murderer who created "Helter Skelter," a racist Armageddon, speaking at his trial.

Ten, fifteen years ago, maybe you could pay a runner seventy-five or a hundred twenty-five dollars a week to run around collecting numbers. Today, you got to pay them three, four hundred dollars for the same work— and this eats up profits.
—Michael "Mad Dog" Tacetta, underboss of the Lucchese crime family.

I don't know the law. I don't know the first thing about it. I've been accused of breaking it.
—Anthony "Tumac" Accetturo, boss of the New Jersey arm of the Lucchese crime family.

I've been in jail all my life.
—Giacomo "Fat Jack" DiNorscio, mobster who acted as his own counsel during his drug trafficking trial, responding to the judge when asked if he had any legal training. DiNorscio was sentenced to 30 years in prison.

This court has not made an intelligent decision during the entire proceedings and I don't expect one now. I don't want mercy. As [executed murderer] Gary Gilmore said, "Let's do it."
—Larry C. Flynt, publisher of *Hustler* magazine, speaking to the judge at his trial for violating obscenity laws in Ohio. He was found guilty.

. . . . I have this certain sense of how things are, this code if you want to use that word, and you believe my code is bull shit. . . . this high-minded crap about the law and the good of society. . . . I happen to believe that that is bull shit.
—Joe N. Gallo, consigliere of the Gambino crime family.

I shall not consent to be tried under a law in which my sex had no voice in making.
—Pearl Hart, believed to be the last person to rob a stagecoach and the only woman ever to do so, speaking to the court during her trial in which she was found guilty and sentenced to jail.

The difference between guilt and innocence in any court is who gets to the judge first with the most.
—Murray Llewellyn Humphreys, a.k.a. "The Camel," Capone-affiliated mobster known for wearing a camel-hair coat and as a "fixer": a man who could grease the path for the mob with the courts, unions, businessmen, etc.

When the time comes to cop a plea, let me know and I will see that you get a good fix.

—Tony Lopoparo, henchman in a Kansas City dope ring, in a wiretapped conversation about finding a favorable judge to sentence his associate Joe Antinori.

law enforcement

I want Rosenthal croaked! Kill him anywhere. Do it in front of a policeman and it will be all right. I'll take care of everything.

—Charles Becker, N.Y.P.D. lieutenant, ordering the killing of the gambler Herman Rosenthal in 1912.

lawyers

They're all crooks. . . . Every last goddamn one of them. All they want is your money.

—Joe N. Gallo, consigliere of the Gambino crime family, on the subject of lawyers.

I wanted to kill them both. I'm glad they're dead. . . . When I entered the courtroom and saw them whispering together to harass me further I could not stand it. When they started to whisper, that was the end.

—Arthur Emil Hansen, a farmer who shot to death two lawyers who had won a civil suit against him, leaving Hansen broke. The shooting occurred in the courtroom.

(hard) lessons

We taught that damn horse of yours a lesson. If you want the saddle, go and get it.

—"Two Guns" Louis Alterie, Chicago bootleg-era gunman, to the owner of the horse that he shot to death after it threw and killed his friend.

lies

She was having her way with me—without my consent.

—Robert Chambers, a.k.a. "The Preppie Murderer," about the woman he strangled to death in New York's Central Park.

This is an honest Administration. We will not go down
on the charge of corruption.

—Robert Haldeman, member of President Richard Nixon's cabinet, paraphrasing Nixon.
Haldeman was convicted of one count of conspiracy, one count of obstruction of justice, and three counts of perjury.

lists

Go to school.
Pull up at mom's house.
Enter/Greet mom.
Go to bathroom.
Prepare knife and handkerchief.
Go directly to mom.
When her back is turned stab until dead.
Cut off her hand.

—Jonathan Eric Cantero, teenager who killed his mother, from his daily list of things
to do.

1. Always look for the widows. Less
   complications.
2. Establish your own background as
   one of wealth and culture.
3. Make friends with the entire family.
4. Send a woman frequent bouquets.
   Roses, never orchids.
5. Don't ask for money. Make her suggest lending it to you.
6. Be attentive at all times.
7. Be gentle and ardent.
8. Always be a perfect gentleman.
   Subordinate sex.

—Sigmund Engel, hustler who claimed to have married 200 women and conned them out of $6 million.
During his trial he gave reporters a list of "dos and don'ts."

Objective: back off.
Strategy: ~~surprise confrontation~~. Communicate seriousness of intent. Communicate seriousness of my intention
and resolve.

—Joseph Robb, a.k.a. "The Killer Tycoon," in a note he wrote to himself outlining his
strategy to deal with the man his wife was having an affair with.

*Interested in welfare schemes. Will contribute to any kind of fund for social betterment.
*Prides himself on his knowledge of art. Will buy any kind of picture if you flatter him into believing he knows all about it.
*Strong on uplift. Will contribute to sociological schemes of all kinds.
*Immensely vain and easy to land for flattering stuff. Likes to have histories of his family written. Easiest lead is to talk genealogy . . . .
—James W. Ryan, a.k.a. "The Postal Kid," a con man who kept a file on all the potential victims for his scams, excerpts from which are quoted above.

I went into the gambling junket operation. We had three things in mind: (1) we wanted to meet suckers, (2) we wanted to make loan sharks out of them, and (3) later we wanted to get them obligated.
—Vincent Teresa, confessed Mafia member, testifying to a Senate sub-committee.

livelihoods

It was exciting and adventurous; robbing banks was my business.
—J. Harvey Bailey, bank robber during the "golden age" of Dillinger, Bonnie and Clyde, et al.

Robbery was my job and I was good at it for some time and then it blew up in my face as I knew it would.
—Basil Banghart, a.k.a. "The Owl," robber and four-time prison escapee of the 1930s, who was known for his large head and eyes and served out his lifelong sentence in Alcatraz prison.

Me? I steal.
—Momo Salvatore "Sam" Giancana, Cosa Nostra overlord of the Chicago area, when asked by Selective Service officials during World War II what his profession was.

Killing men is my business.
—Tom Horn, a former lawman who turned hired gun and killed cattle rustlers for a living, until he was hanged for killing a 14-year-old boy by mistake.

Why, after I'd made my rep, some of the Chicago Syndicate wanted me to work for them as a hood--you know, handle a machine gun. They offered me $250 a week and all the protection I needed. I was on the lam at the time and not able to work at my regular line. But I couldn't consider it. "I'm a thief," I said. "I'm no lousy hoodlum."
—Alvin "Creepy" Karpis, freelance criminal not associated with any mob, telling the FBI why that was so.

I saw nothing wrong in killing for money. If I had not done it someone else would.
—Marlin "Big Soul" Rivera, a hired killer believed to have murdered over 50 people and known for decapitating his victims.

Why did I rob banks? Because I enjoyed it. I loved it. I was more alive when I was inside a bank, robbing it, than any other time in my life. I enjoyed everything about it so much that one or two weeks later I'd be out looking for the next job.
—William "The Actor" Sutton, bank robber known for his disguises and prison breakouts.

I had no feelings. . . . It just became another job. In the evening we never discussed our work, but just drank and played cards.
—Gustav Wagner, Deputy Nazi Commandant of the Sobobor extermination camp in Poland, on his feelings about killing at the camp.

I'm no undertaker.
—Frankie Yale, Brooklyn mob leader, responding to the police when they asked how he made his living.

location

I think I'm standing on her now.
—Peter Thomas Anthony Manuel, who admitted to murdering two 17-year-old girls, after leading police to the place where he buried their bodies.

Our beautiful Hawaiian isle is, for us, worse than Alcatraz.
Alcatraz at least gives free room and board.
—Imelda Marcos, wife of the corrupt de facto dictator of the Philippines, President
Ferdinand Marcos, remarking on their life in exile in 1988.

love

I loved you too much . . . that was my problem. . . . I
loved you too much.
—O. J. Simpson, star football player turned actor/ad man and known wife beater, suspected but acquitted of murdering his ex-wife and her friend, addressing the coffin of
his ex-wife at her funeral.

loyalty

If I knew who killed Deanie, I'd
shoot it out with the gang of killers before the sun rose in the morning and some of us, maybe all of
us, would be lying on slabs in the
undertaker's place
—"Two Guns" Louis Alterie, Chicago bootleg-era gangster known for carrying two .38 caliber guns, speaking about the killing of his boss Dion "Deanie" O'Bannion.

Oh, the KGB.
—Aldrich Ames, CIA agent secretly working for the KGB, on whether he felt more loyal
to the CIA or the KGB.

May I burn in hell if I betray my friends and family.
—George Fresolone, member of the Bruno/Scarfo crime family who turned police informant, on the oath that made him a member of the family. Later he " . . . vowed that
someday I would bring them down."

If tomorrow I go wrong, I want you to hit me in the
head too.
—Vito Genovese, head of the Genovese crime family, referring to the need to kill fellow
New Jersey mobster Willie Moretti, because it was feared that Moretti's advanced case of
syphilis was causing him to talk too much and jeopardizing the secrecy of the Mafia.

The National Socialism of all of us is anchored in uncriti-
cal loyalty, in the surrender to the führer that does not
ask for the why in individual cases, in the silent execution of his orders.
—Rudolf Hess, Deputy Leader of the Nazi Party.

. . . once you got hooked up with people—well, that is it . . . you are with them for life. After these guys got sent to jail, I was still sending envelopes every month to them. Well, to their wives.

—Vincent Teresa, confessed Mafia member, talking about the "cut" that he would receive from his operators and then send on to his bosses.

the mafia

We're big business without the top hats.

—Anonymous colleague of Al Capone, on organized crime.

The government seems to have this cockamamy idea that there's this thing called the Mafia, and the Mafia goes around corrupting perfectly honest and upstanding people. Gimme a break!

—Joe N. Gallo, consigliere of the Gambino crime family.

The law's gonna be tough on us, okay: If they don't put us away . . . for one year or two, that's all we need. . . . But if I get a year, [I'm] gonna put this thing together where they could never break it, never destroy it. Even if we die, be a good thing.

—John Gotti, boss of the Gambino crime family, from a conversation taped by the FBI. In the background another mobster in the room could be heard saying, "It's a helluva legacy to leave." Gotti then continued, "Well, you know why it would be, ah, because it would be right. Maybe after 30 years it would deteriorate, but it would take that long to fuckin' succumb."

We're bigger than U.S. Steel.

—Meyer Lansky, underworld financial whiz and a founder of the national crime syndicate, on the size of the Mafia.

We're not crazed killers, at least I didn't think we were at the time.

—Philip Leonetti, Philadelphia-based Mafia underboss.

We were respectable people.

—Philip Leonetti, Philadelphia-based Mafia underboss, on Mafia ethics.

They call anybody a mob who makes six percent or more on money.

—Willie Moretti, a.k.a. Willie Moore, New Jersey Syndicate boss, testifying at Senate hearings on organized crime.

manners

I prefer to pay for my breakfast. I only will let you pay for my funeral.

—George Paul Hetenyi, a New York State reverend who killed his wife, speaking to the sheriff during the breakfast they had together before going to view Hetenyi's wife's body.

Thank you very much. Don't forget my house in Deal if you are down on the shore. You are invited.

—Willie Moretti, a.k.a. Willie Moore, New Jersey Syndicate boss, testifying at Senate hearings on organized crime, after being told by Senator Charles Toby that his testimony was frank and "rather refreshing."

It was nothing personal, sir.

—Luigi Ronsisvalle, Brooklyn-based Mafia hit man turned federal witness, explaining his general feelings on killing people.

marriage

I never heard of Richard Morton. . . . Oh, that Richard Morton! . . . . Yes, I was married to him.

—Nannie Doss, Oklahoma woman who murdered eleven people, including four of her five husbands.

Marriage was purely a business proposition to me. When I found they had money I went after that.

—Johann Hoch, Chicago man who married as many as three times per year, then poisoned his wives and took their money.

At times I've felt like a battered boyfriend or husband.

—O. J. Simpson, star football player turned actor/ad man and known wife beater, suspected but acquitted of murdering his ex-wife and her friend.

masochism

So why don't you stop hurting so many women, and just concentrate on hurting me?

—Jean Harris, school headmistress, to her lover, the Scarsdale Diet Doctor, Herman Tarnower, who she later murdered.

If only pain were not so painful!

—Albert Howard Fish, sadomasochistic child killer, commenting after inserting needles under his own fingernails, something he practiced regularly. It took two throws of the switch to kill him in the electric chair; there was a short circuit due to all the old needles lodged in his body.

medicine

I'm going to make you feel better.
—Richard Angelo, registered nurse at a Long Island, New York, hospital, to a patient, just before adding a lethal drug to his intravenous tube. The patient almost died and was left paralyzed.

Oh, come look what I've done, sweetheart.
—Martha Beck, registered nurse, swindler, and murderer, to her con artist boyfriend änd partner in crime, Raymond Fernandez, as she held the daughter of one of her adult victims under water, drowning her.

The time is not far distant when I shall be able to say that one doctor, with, perhaps, ten assistants can probably effect several hundred, if not one thousand sterilizations on a single day.
—Karl Clauberg, Nazi "doctor" who performed experiments on concentration camp victims.

They can't get me for murder. All I did was commit malpractice.
—Hans Graewe, a.k.a. "The Surgeon," hit man for a Cleveland, Ohio, gang who was known for his expertise at cutting up bodies.

I have been like an angel of mercy to them.
—Anna Marie Hahn, when faced with the overwhelming evidence that she poisoned two elderly men in her care in order to collect insurance money.

My mission is to heal and help the sick.
—Antoinette Scieri, a private nurse who fatally poisoned at least five of her patients in 1920s France.

men

All is dust and lies. So much the worse for the men who get in my way. Men are mere stepping-stones to me. As soon as they begin to fail or are played out, I put them scornfully aside. Society is a vast chessboard, men the pawns, some white, some black; I move them as I please, and break them when they bore me.
—Jeanne Brecourt, 19th-century French courtesan and blackmailer who hired a henchman to blind her lover with acid in an effort to enslave him to her.

mental health

He's been crazy all his life. He's not just, you know, a little funny. He's really nuts.
—anonymous mobster on Mafioso Giacomo "Fat Jack" DiNorscio, who was convicted of drug trafficking and sentenced to 30 years in prison.

messes

It's done. It's the messiest yet. It normally takes one blow.
—Ian Brady, 28-year-old Englishman, after bludgeoning a man to death.

I just pulled the trigger and blood flew everywhere. Oh boy! I never seen so much blood!
—Walter Kelbach, who, along with his lover, Myron Lance, killed six people in December of 1966, speaking to a television reporter about one of his killings.

Pep ain't gonna like his garage all messed up like this.
—Harry "Happy" Maione, killer for Murder, Inc., assessing the splattered blood on the walls and floor after gunning down mobster Joe Amberg and his driver in a garage owned by Harry "Pep" Strauss.

metaphors and similes

Our position is similar to that of the English nation. We in the racing field own three-quarters of the globe and manage the balance. In other words, the few little nations that are left have to pay us tribute to continue. Now why isn't that the most beautiful and most satisfactory position to be in which ought to satisfy even me.
—Moe Annenberg, 1920s mobster active in horse racing.

I had no more thought of right or wrong than a wolf that prowls the prairie.
—Jack Black, professional burglar from 1870 to 1900 who eventually went straight, ending up as a reporter for a newspaper.

[Mobsters] go through girlfriends like veal cutlets.
—Joseph "Joey" Canatlupo, Colombo crime family associate turned government witness.

The age of a woman does not mean a thing . . . after all, the best tunes are played on the oldest fiddles.
—Sigmund Engel, hustler who claimed to have married 200 women and conned them out of $6 million, speaking to reporters on the way to jail.

It was like in World War II. They tell you to go to the draft board and sign up. Well, I signed up.
—Santo Trafficante, Tampa, Florida, Mafia boss, on the CIA's efforts to recruit the Mafia to assassinate Cuban leader Fidel Castro in the 1960s.

methods

The way I done it, I seen it done on a TV show. I had my own way, though. Simple and easy. No one would hear them scream.
—Christine Falling, a Florida babysitter who admitted to killing three of her charges by suffocation, describing her methods.

Ocean front rooms and great meals on bad plastic. That's how a wise guy goes on vacation.
—George Fresolone, member of the Bruno/Scarfo crime family, on the high life with stolen credit cards.

If you think it will be better or quicker, then use a knife but the job must be done.
—Marlene Lehnberg, a 19-year-old would-be model who bribed a pauper to kill her lover's wife, from a letter telling the murderer how to go about it.

. . . closing my eyes, I gave him a tremendous blow on the head. . . . The man screamed in such a way that I will never forget as long as I live. His scream was . . . very long, infinitely long, and it still seems to me as if that scream were piercing my brains.
—Ramon Mercader, an agent of Soviet dictator Joseph Stalin's secret police, describing how he murdered the Bolshevik revolutionary Leon Trotsky in 1940.

They had it down to a science. You walked in, you got shot in the head with a silencer, somebody wrapped a towel around your head to stop the blood from going all over the place . . . [someone would] stab you in the heart to stop the heart from pumping so the blood would stop. Then you were hung upside down in the shower and your neck was cut, and you bled for about forty minutes. And then they had pool tarpaulins and regular butcher kits with the saws that butchers used. And they would just take you apart, put you in garbage bags, put you in boxes, put you out in the dumpster, call for pick up and you were in the dump. By the next day there was twenty tons of garbage on top of you.
—Dominick Montiglio, former Gambino crime family associate, on the subject of waste disposal.

. . . . I gave him a glass of beer which contained arsenic. . . . It was several day before he died. I made up my mind that the next one would not cause that much trouble.
—Frederick Mors, a porter at a home for the elderly, who poisoned 17 of its inhabitants from 1914 to 1915.

. . . first I committed sodomy on him and then I killed him. . . . His brains were coming out of his ears when I left him and he will never be any deader.
—Carl Panzram, misanthropic mass murderer, describing how he killed a 12-year-old boy while he was working for an oil company in Africa. Initially sentenced to 25 years in prison, Panzram killed again while incarcerated and was executed in 1930.

I iron-whipped him with all the pent-up hate and fury of a warped childhood again coming out of me! I clubbed, raked and hammered his face until it was a bloody pulp.
—Morris "Red" Rudensky, a.k.a. Max Motel Friedman, robber, expert safecracker, and escape artist, describing what he did to a gangster who wanted a bigger share of a robbery.

I had to make them mad at me first, antagonize them. I had to do something to them . . . yeah, provoke them so they were helpless. . . . Then we would start shooting, Bang! Bang! Bang! Looking back, it was rough.
—Mike Tyson, heavyweight champion boxer convicted of rape, on his childhood life of crime.

I used to insert tubes of typhoid, pneumonia, and diphtheria in his soups and rice pudding. Once I gave him a nasty nasal spray filled with tuberculosis bacteria. Still nothing happened. I tried to give him pneumonia by putting water in his Wellingtons, damping his sheets, opening his bedroom window and wetting the seat of the automobile before taking him out for a drive.
—Dr. Arthur Warren Waite, New York dentist who killed his in-laws in an attempt to inherit their estate, describing his techniques.

mistakes

Home . . . and ain't that a helluva place for it?
—Arthur "Doc" Barker, bank robber and murderer, when caught by the FBI and asked where his gun was.

You can imagine my embarrassment when I killed the wrong guy.
—Joseph Valachi, a henchman in the Genovese crime family, on the murder of John Joseph Saupp, a fellow prison inmate who Valachi mistakenly thought was going to kill him.

modesty

[My brothers and I] buried 20 Irishmen to take this town over. We can't begin to dig up half we got rid of. And I'm not bragging either.
—Gennaro "Jerry" Angiulo, Boston Mafia boss, on the mob situation in Boston in the 1960s.

A lot of men can buy all these local people. But it is not easy to buy the whole district.
—Hastings Kamuzu Banda, 20th-century president-for-life of Malawi.

Women dream often of chivalry, but seldom get any . . . a field in which my luster is undimmed.
—Sigmund Engel, hustler who claimed to have married 200 women and conned them out of $6 million, speaking to reporters during his trial.

mom

What's my mother going to think?
—Robert Chambers, a.k.a. "The Preppie Murderer," while confessing to killing his prep school classmate, Jennifer Levin, during what he called "rough sex" in New York's Central Park.

One of things that makes this case difficult is we included [murdered] my mom.
—Lyle Menendez, convicted with his brother Eric for shooting to death both their parents.

mood swings

I'm a manic depressive. Sometimes I think I'm fucking superman and sometimes I can't get out of bed.
—Tommy Agro, "soldier" (i.e. bodyguard, hit man) for the Gambino crime family.

For an instant a strange feeling, as of shame, comes over me; but the next moment I'm filled with anger at the sentiment, so unworthy of a revolutionist. With defiant hatred I look him full in the face.
—Alexander Berkman, anarchist, recollecting his thoughts after his unsuccessful assassination attempt on Henry Clay Frick, chairman of the Carnegie Steel Company, during which Berkman shot Frick twice in the neck.

I have a small part in me that cannot understand the world and what goes on in it. I did not want to kill anybody, and I really don't know why I did. . . .
—Mark David Chapman, man who shot and killed former Beatle John Lennon in 1980.

I stood there and looked at her . . . something like clicked in me . . . and then I remember stabbing her in the stomach. And then I stabbed her in the chest. . . .
—Paula Cooper, 15-year-old who stabbed to death a 78-year-old Bible teacher.

I can only say that I have had a brain storm.
—Miles Giffard, 27-year-old Briton who murdered his parents and threw their bodies into the ocean in Cornwall, from his statement to the police.

My God, I've gone bananas . . . When are the paramedics coming? I don't know these women.
—Jeffrey Joseph Gurga, a former county prosecutor in Illinois who stabbed a woman to death and injured her daughter, to a neighbor as he tried to escape the crime scene.

I hadn't decided on anything. But suddenly I had a strange impulse to end it all . . . for both of us.
—Betty Hardaker, a California woman who killed her five-year-old daughter, for no apparent reason, when they were out for a walk in February of 1940.

I'm a Dr. Jekyll and Mr. Hyde. I killed! I killed!
—Edward Joseph Leonski, Texas GI, to his friends. He confessed to having murdered
three women while stationed in Australia in 1942.

I felt hellish and very peculiar inside.
—Patrick Mackay, murderer of three, on murdering.

morality

I would kill a Turk, but I wouldn't torture them.
—Anonymous Serbian priest expressing disapproval of the torture of Muslims.

They keep bringing up my six other husbands. What's that got to do with today's love? . . . They were all about Mr. Birch's age when I married them. So what? I done the decent thing. You never heard of Pearl Choate not marrying a man. Pearl Choate don't shack up!
—Pearl Choate, Texas nurse who married six rich, over 90-year-old men, all of whom died in her care.
Choate served 12 years in prison for shooting one of them to death.

I guess our senses of morality are different.
—Patricia Columbo, 19-year-old woman who brutally killed her parents and younger
brother, speaking to the police about pornographic photos of sex acts that included
herself, her boyfriend, and the family dog.

We wouldn't go out and kill little kids.
—Philip Leonetti, Philadelphia-based Mafia underboss, on Mafia ethics.

I may not be the most moral and upright man who lives
but I have never stooped so low as to become involved
in prostitution.
—Charles "Lucky" Luciano, mobster who was found guilty of dozens of prostitution
related crimes.

In a sense, the way I believe it, you give to me $30,000,
and I am sent to kill a person. You kill him, not me. But
to move pounds of heroin, you destroy hundreds of
thousands of young American generations. That makes
me shake.
—Luigi Ronsisvalle, Brooklyn-based Mafia hit man turned federal witness, on the ethics
of being a paid killer.

The old-time confidence man had a saying: "Never send them to the river." We never picked on poor people or cleaned them out completely. Taking the life savings from poor old women is just the same as putting a revolver to her head and pressing the trigger.
—Joseph "Yellow Kid" Weil, early 20th-century hustler who claimed to have conned 2,000 people out of more than $3 million, talking about the "code of honor" in his "profession."

movies

"Jaws" is the warmest, tenderest, lovingest movie of the year. I give it four coconuts.
—Idi Amin, 1970s Ugandan general/dictator, on the movie *Jaws.*

"The Three Little Pigs."
—John Dillinger, infamous bank robber of the 1920s and '30s, when asked which movie was his favorite.

Carmine Galante: I saw Casablanca, the movie, and I saw a girl.
Police Detective: John Wayne was very good in Casablanca.
Galante: Not so good.
Detective: What's the girl's name?
Galante: I don't know. She was not so good either.
—Carmine Galante, a.k.a. "Mr. Lilo," mobster in the Bonnano crime family, being interrogated about his whereabouts on the night of a murder, for which he was a prime suspect.

You North Germans are so humorless about your anti-Semitism.
—Gottfried Kussel, "The Austrian führer" of neo-Nazis, explaining to his German comrades how it was that *The Blues Brothers,* on which many Jews worked, could be his favorite movie.

multi-culturalism

That was a good hunt. There were a lot of rabbits here.
—Anonymous Serbian soldier, while looking over a field piled with the bodies of Muslims.

Russia needs Armenia, but she has no need of Armenians.
—Anonymous Tsarist minister.

The Slavs are to work for us. In so far as we do not need
them, they may die. Slav fertility is not desirable.
—Martin Bormann, Head of the Nazi Party Chancellery and Hitler's private secretary,
in a memo.

Fuck the Chinese, fuck the Jews, and fuck the fucking
Paisans who are grabbing more than their share. It's our
association to reap the benefits.
—Paul Castellano, a.k.a. "Big Paul," Mafia boss in the Gambino family.

We say there is a conspiracy against every Italian-American.
—Joe Columbo, boss of his own crime family, during his campaign against
ethnic slurs.

We have every kind of mixture you can have. I have a
black, I have a woman, two Jews, and a cripple.
—James G. Watt, Ronald Reagan's interior secretary, who pleaded guilty to a misdemeanor charge of trying to influence a federal grand jury, speaking about the composition of a coal advisory panel.

musicians

Me and the boys will pay them horn tooters a visit, one visit, and take the joint over.
—Samuel "Samoots" Amatuna, Chicago Mafioso and one-time professional fiddle player, believed to be
the first gangster to carry his gun in a violin case, on a strategy for taking over the musicians union.

I gave him some more poison. Suddenly I remembered
how splendidly my boy used to sing in church, so I said,
"Sing, my boy! Sing my favorite song!" He sang it with
his lovely clear voice, then suddenly he cried out, gripped
his stomach, gasped, and was dead.
—Marie Kardos, a Hungarian women who poisoned her husband, lover, and her son,
about whom she was speaking at her murder trial

nostalgia

The sight of the flames delighted me, but above all it was the excitement of the attempts to extinguish the fire and the agitation of those who saw their property being destroyed.
—Peter Kürten, a.k.a. "The Düsseldorf Vampire," who drank the blood of some of his nine murder victims and sexually assaulted at least 23 other people, recalling his early days as an arsonist.

I get tears in my eyes just thinking about all the things that have happened . . . and all the guys that got killed. . . . And all the guys that got killed were good guys . . . .
—Joseph "The Nodder" Sodano, Scarfo crime family mobster who specialized in bookmaking operations, speaking about some of his fellow mobsters.

Remember how I liked to pour some of the blood out of them?
—Ottis Toole, an arsonist and serial killer, speaking to his partner, Henry Lee Lucas, in a telephone conversation taped by the police. Toole was known to have practiced cannibalism. Together, Toole and Lucas are believed to have murdered 108 people.

objection!

I'm no robber. I took the money and the cash register because I wanted to see how it worked.
—Edward Gein, a farmer who exhumed graves in order to "research" and sometimes eat female anatomy, and who ultimately killed two women. He objected to being charged with robbery in addition to murder.

We are not assassins! We did not stab our husbands. We did not hang them or drown them either! They died from poison and this was a pleasant death for them!
—Lydia Olah, a member of a Hungarian murder ring in which women were poisoning their husbands to death, shouting out to the court during her trial.

the obvious

I grew up with guns. They didn't make me feel powerful but I knew that I could get my way by having one in my hand.
—Basil Banghart, a.k.a. "The Owl," robber and four-time prison escapee of the 1930s, who was known for his large head and eyes and served out his lifelong sentence in Alcatraz prison.

We dug a hole in Michigan and dropped him in and covered the hole with lime. I don't think anybody's going to come across Doc Moran again.

—Fred Barker, murderer, bank robber, and son of the infamous Ma Barker, on the doctor he had killed. Dr. Moran had botched the plastic surgery on Fred Barker's face and fingertips that was supposed to hide his identity. Moran made the mistake of bragging to the madam of a whorehouse that he was going to turn in the Barker gang.

I saw the look in Jimmy's face, and knew my time had come. . . . Now, you don't gotta be a science guy to figure out I'm in a lot of trouble here. They were going to kill me. . . . They started killing each other. I mean, it got really nuts.

—Billie Beattie, Westies gang member.

I guess you don't think much of me.

—Richard Carpenter, robber and police killer, to a family he was holding hostage at gunpoint.

Well, it's all over now.

—Lee Harvey Oswald, who assassinated President John F. Kennedy on November 22, 1963, upon finding that his gun had run out of bullets as he tried to fire on police officers later that day.

Because that's where the money is.

—William "The Actor" Sutton, 20th-century bank robber known for his disguises and prison escapes, when asked why he robbed banks.

odds

Seven out of ten times when we hit a guy, we're wrong. But the other three times we hit, we make up for it.

—Statement attributed to Momo Salvatore "Sam" Giancana, Cosa Nostra overlord of the Chicago area.

orders

Nice and easy or I'll blow your head off.

—Clyde Barrow, bank robber of "Bonnie and Clyde" fame, to deputy sheriff Joe Johns, after taking him hostage.

Listen, I'll cut—you wrap.

—Roy di Meo, a "capo" (captain) in the Gambino crime family, to his men who were
taking too long to dismember the body of a victim. The victim was the son-in-law of
Mafia boss Paul Castellano. Castellano ordered the hit because his son-in-law was
unfaithful to Castellano's daughter.

From his grave he ordered the hit.

—Joe DiVarco, a.k.a. "Little Caesar," mobster, relating that deceased Mafioso "Milwaukee Phil" Aldirisio
would have wanted a certain bookmaker dead because the bookie wanted to marry Aldirisio's mistress.

. . . And from now on, I'm telling you if a guy just so
mentions "La" . . . he just says "La," the guy, I'm gonna
strangle the cock sucker. You know what I mean? He
don't have to say "Cosa Nostra," just "La" and they go.

—John Gotti, boss of the Gambino crime family, on how to keep mobsters from talking about the mob or "La Cosa Nostra."

Just destroy all the tapes.

—Richard Nixon, speaking in 1986 on what he learned from the Watergate scandal that
brought down his presidency.

Make 'a him go away.

—Paul "The Waiter" Ricca, Chicago Outfit mob leader, uttering his standard phrase
for giving the order to have someone murdered.

[Take him on] a one-way ride.

—Hymie Weiss, O'Banion gang boss, giving his order to kill.

outrage

Why'd they tell me he's even been carrying a gun? Can
you tie that—a confidence man lugging artillery! What
for? To tap wires with? Or deal seconds off a deck of
cards? I'm telling you we've got to clean house! Got to
throw out these people who are ruining our profession.

—Anonymous con man, lamenting about the decline of the "pure" con.

I'm telling you, it's murder.

—Willie Obront, Cotroni crime family money launderer, on the subject of
police wiretapping.

That is my bullet.
—John Nepomuk Schrank, former saloon owner who shot President Theodore Roosevelt because he had a dream in which the ghost of Roosevelt's predecessor, William McKinley, accused Roosevelt of his murder, saying: "Let not a murderer take the presidential chair. Avenge my death." Schrank became enraged when he discovered that the bullet he fired at the president remained in his chest and could not be donated to the New York Historical Society, where he wanted it put on display.

overkill

I had caused my uncle and aunt so much heartache that I decided I'd done wrong to them and I thought giving them poison was the best way to right that wrong and save them from further hurt.
—Leroy Drake, a.k.a. "Pious Leroy," murderer whose devoutly religious aunt and uncle became depressed when Drake was arrested for the theft of a car. Drake claimed he sought to relieve them of their depression by killing them.

You've got me on five. What good would 50 more do?
—Herman Drenth, a Virginia man convicted of killing five women, but who may have been responsible for murdering as many as 50, when finally caught by the police.

You don't look too bad—here's another.
—Bernhard H. Goetz, an electrical engineering consultant known as "The Subway Vigilante" and a hero to some, while shooting one of four men he claimed were going to rob him on a New York City subway car in 1984.

I've killed so many I'm unable to remember them all.
—Arnfinn Nesset, Norwegian serial killer believed to have killed as many as 62 people.

Sure I killed him. This is his suit I'm wearing now.
—Kenneth Neu, a would-be nightclub singer, confessing to the murder of Lawrence Shead.

Maybe a dozen. Maybe more. I try to put those things out of my mind.
—Daniel Lee Siebert, an art teacher turned killer, when asked by the police how many murders he had committed.

I'd have killed a thousand if I'd had bullets enough.
—Howard Unruh, army sharpshooter who shot 13 people to death in a 12-minute rampage in Camden, New Jersey, in 1949.

I did one and I thought I just might as well go on. I planned to kill maybe a dozen or so. I was fed up. I was broke. I thought I'd better get some money somehow.
—Dennis Whitney, Californian who killed seven people in a cross-country murder spree.

parting thoughts

And you can go to hell, hell, hell!
—William Bonney, a.k.a. "Billy the Kid," legendary outlaw of the Old West, responding to the judge who sentenced him to hang until ". . . you are dead, dead, dead!"

Sic semper tyrannis! (Ever thus to tyrants). . . . The South is avenged!
—John Wilkes Booth, actor who assassinated President Abraham Lincoln in 1865, shouting from the stage of Ford's Theater after the shooting.

You old bastard, I hope you die screaming of cancer.
—John Bowden, convicted murderer, yelling at the judge during his trial.

Vive la revolution! Vive l'anarchie!
—Santo Caserio, Italian anarchist, as he stabbed the president of France in 1894.

Death itself isn't dreadful, but hanging seems an awkward way of entering the adventure.
—Gerald Chapman, jewel thief, robber, and murderer, who killed a policeman during his last robbery, on his impending death by hanging.

I done my duty!
—Leon Czolgosz, the 28-year-old laborer who shot and killed President William McKinley in 1901, immediately after firing.

I hope forked lightening [sic] will strike every one of you bastards dead!
—Jack Gallagher, a.k.a. "Three-Fingered Jack," Old West outlaw, to the vigilantes who were about to hang him in 1864.

To me, death is better than serving time in Indiana.
—Anthony Goodin, a drifter sentenced to life imprisonment for the murder of a Georgia schoolteacher, speaking as he waived extradition proceedings.

You are all low, consummate jackasses!
—Charles J. Guiteau, assassin of President James A. Garfield, addressing the jury at his murder trial after the guilty verdict was announced.

I'll be in hell before you start breakfast, boys!
—"Black Jack" Ketchum, train robber, shouting to the throng gathered at his hanging. An incorrectly tied rope caused Ketchum's head to be ripped from his body when the trap door opened.

Al, we've got to put an end to this obsession.
—Dennis Sweeny, a one-time volunteer for the Student Nonviolent Coordinating Committee, speaking to his college mentor, Allard Lowenstein, moments before shooting him to death.

We killed together, so we expect to die together.
—George R. York and James D. Latham, teenage U.S. Army privates who went AWOL in 1959 and then killed seven people, speaking to the court after they were sentenced to death.

passions

Sometimes I see a stranger who looks like easy money. Sometimes a fellow with 'good thing' printed all over him struts into my hotel. Then the old feeling rises up under my vest and makes me itch to get at him.
—Will Irwin, early-20th-century con man.

Every man has his passion. Some prefer whist. I prefer killing people.
—Rudolf Pleil, a German man convicted of nine rape/murders, who called himself Germany's "champion death maker."

patriotism

We won't stand for this. We are Americans.
—Anthony Anastasio, Mafioso whose crime family controlled the docks in South Brooklyn, Hoboken, and Staten Island, dismissing the suggestion that all longshoremen were gangsters.

It must be a greater honor to be a street-cleaner and citizen of this Reich than a king in a foreign state.
—Adolf Hitler in *Mein Kampf*.

pick-up lines

Miss, I have a bomb in my suitcase and I want you to sit beside me.
—Dan B. Cooper, skyjacker, to a stewardess on a 1971 flight from Portland, Oregon, to Seattle, Washington.

piety

Before I began counterfeiting I deliberately had my name
stricken form the Christian Endeavor rolls.
—John L.T. Cooper, soldier convicted of manufacturing counterfeit $10 gold coins,
suggesting to the judge that he deserved a lenient sentence.

I had no intention to kill the king. I might have done this
had I been so inclined. I did it only that God might touch
the king's heart, and work on him to restore things to
their former footing.
—Robert François Damiens, who stabbed King Louis XV of France in 1857, to protest the king's stand in the struggle between orthodox Catholics and the Jansenists.

pity

"Why don't you get up and stop faking?"
—Mildred Mary Bolton, to her husband as he tried to crawl away after she had shot
him six times.

One less German in Paris!
—Jeanne Brecourt, 19th-century French courtesan, upon learning a former lover had
committed suicide.

plans

This is the day I will kill someone. If I meet anyone that
will be it.
—Penny Bjorkland, an 18-year-old, on the day she murdered a gardener.

I'm going to live by the gun and roam.
—William Cook, early 1950s robber and murderer, when asked by his father about his
future plans.

I'm going to get me a couple of Mormons.
—Gary Gilmore, first person executed in the U.S. following the reinstatement of the
death penalty, while in prison for robbery, a year-and-a-half before he shot and killed
two Mormon men while committing another robbery.

Ten days from now.

—Tillie Klimek, Chicago woman who poisoned to death her five husbands in order to collect their life
insurance policies, upon being asked by a stranger when her husband had died. Klimek was buying a
dress to wear to his funeral.

I used to spend all my time figuring how I could murder the most people with the least harm and expense to myself, and I finally thought of a way to kill off a whole town. . . .
—Carl Panzram, misanthropic mass murderer who schemed to bomb trains and contaminate reservoirs. Initially sentenced to 25 years in prison, Panzram killed again while incarcerated and was executed in 1930.

[I'm going to] . . . kill someone tonight just for luck.
—Samuel Strawhim, gun slinger of the Old West.

pleas

Shoot me. Don't take me in for junk. Let me run, and then shoot me!
—Waxey Gordon, Prohibition-era bootlegger who was left penniless after income tax evasion penalties and imprisonment, to the police after he was arrested for dealing in narcotics (junk).

Don't shoot G-Man! I've been waiting for you.
—George "Machine Gun" Kelly, bank robber and kidnapper of the 1920s and '30s, expressing his apparent relief upon being captured.

Whoever has my children, please, please bring them back.
—Susan Smith, South Carolina mother who later confessed to killing her two sons by strapping them into their car seats and rolling the car into a lake.

pleasure

I don't mind people getting hurt because I just like to watch it.
—Walter Kelbach, who, along with his lover, Myron Lance, killed six people in December of 1966.

Get some morphine, dearie, and we'll go out in the ward. You and I will have a lot of fun seeing them die.
—Jane Toppan, Massachusetts nurse who confessed to killing 31 people, speaking to a visitor at the state insane asylum where she spent the rest of her life.

You know something, I like to hurt women when I make love to them. I like to hear them scream with pain, to see them bleed. It gives me pleasure.
—Mike Tyson, heavyweight champion boxer who was convicted of raping a beauty pageant contestant.

poetry

You've lost your job,
You've lost your dough,
Your jewels and handsome houses.
But things could be worse, you know.
You haven't lost your trousers.
—An anonymous note left by Chicago gangsters next to the body of "Machine Gun" Jack McGurn, a hit man for Al Capone's mob. McGurn was lying in a pool of his own blood in a bowling alley.

I've labored long and hard for bread,
For honor and for riches
But on my corns too long you've tread,
You fine-haired sons-of-bitches.
—Charles E. Bolton, a.k.a. "Black Bart", stagecoach and train robber, in a note to the posse of lawmen on his trail after he robbed a Wells Fargo stagecoach in 1877.

Here I lay me down to sleep
To wait the coming morrow,
Perhaps success, perhaps defeat
And everlasting sorrow,
Yet come what will, I'll try it once
My conditions can't be worse,
And if there's money in that box,
'Tis money in my purse.
—Charles E. Bolton, a.k.a. "Black Bart," stagecoach and train robber, in a note left for lawmen after a heist in 1878.

So here I've stood while wind and rain
Have set the trees a sobbin'
And risked my life for that damned stage
That wasn't worth the robbin'
—Charles E. Bolton, a.k.a. "Black Bart," stagecoach and train robber, in a note attributed to him after a Wells Fargo coach was robbed in 1888.

If your father were alive
How unhappy he would be.
To hear the vicious lies
Being told about me.
—Mary Faye Craft, in a poem to her stepchildren, shortly before she was convicted of killing their father.

Countless cons, with writs galore,
A horde of deadly dingbats;
Guilty as hell, but still they yell
"We wanna change our habitats."
—Joseph Paul "Dutch" Cretzer, bank robber also known as a prison escape artist, who
died during a 1946 attempted breakout from Alcatraz that turned into a riot.

Twenty-one defendants are here today
The scales of justice they're hoping to sway.
Charged with RICO and organized crime,
A law which makes justice truly more blind.
—Gerald DeLuca, mobster tried for racketeering and drug trafficking, from a poem he
wrote during a lull in his trial.

I am going to the Lordy, I am so
glad . . .
I saved my party and my land; glory,
hallelujah . . .
But they have murdered me for it,
and that is the reason
I am going to the Lordy . . .
—Charles J. Guiteau, assassin of President James A. Garfield, reciting a poem he had written on the
occasion of his hanging.

'Twas the night before Christmas when in part of the house,
Arthur was snuggling with Vivian, his spouse.
In the guest room lay Herman, who, trying to sleep,
was counting the broads in his life 'stead of sheep!
—Jean Harris, the school headmistress who murdered her lover, Herman Tarnower, the
Scarsdale Diet Doctor.

Now Bonnie and Clyde are the Barrow gang
I'm sure you all have read
How they rob and steal
And those who squeal
Are usually found dying or dead . . .

If a policeman is killed in Dallas
And they have no clues to guide—
If they can't find a fiend,
They just wipe the slate clean,
And hang it on Bonnie and Clyde . . .

This road was so dimly lighted
There were no highway signs to guide,
But they made up their minds
If the roads were all blind
They wouldn't give up till they died . . .

They don't think they are too tough or desperate,
They know the law always wins,
They have been shot at before
But they do not ignore
That death is the wages of sin . . .

Some day they'll go down together;
And they'll bury them side by side;
To few it'll be grief—
To the law a relief—
But it's death for Bonnie and Clyde.
—excerpts from "The Story of Suicide Sal," by Bonnie Parker, of the "Bonnie and Clyde" bank robbing duo.

The police haven't got the report yet,
But Clyde called me up today;
He said,
"Don't start any fights—We aren't working nights—
We're joining the NRA."
—Limerick by Bonnie Parker, of the "Bonnie and Clyde" bank robbing duo. The NRA was the New Deal Program.

I don't intend to serve this out,
Or even let despair
Deprive me of my liberty
Or give me one gray hair.
—Oliver Curtis Perry, New York-born ex-cowboy turned train robber, from a note left on his bed after he escaped from a hospital for the criminally insane in 1895.

You've blackened and besmeared a mother,
Once a man's plaything—a toy—
What have you gained by all you've said?
And has it-brought you joy?
—Ruth May Brown Snyder, bored, nymphomanical housewife who, with the help of her lover, Henry Judd Gray, murdered her husband; from a poem she wrote lambasting the press for their ugly portrayal of her.

politics as usual

I'll be the guy to break your legs!
—Hugh J. Addonizio, 1960s mayor of Newark, New Jersey, who took payoffs from the Mafia and was convicted on conspiracy charges, speaking to a candidate running against him.

The city charges, the sheriff charges, and the mayor charges. They just won't let you make any money.
—Joe Antinori, Kansas City dope ring henchman.

Yeah? How much money can you spend?
—Bobby Baker, secretary to the majority of the U.S.Senate, speaking to the chief lobbyist for the U.S. Savings and Loan League about a plan to pay Oklahoma Senator Robert Kerr $400,000 to kill a tax increase for the savings and loan industry.

This memorandum addresses the matter of how we can maximize the fact of our incumbency in dealing with persons known to be active in their opposition to our Administration. Stated a bit more bluntly—how we can use the available federal machinery to screw our political enemies.
—John Dean, a special counsel to President Nixon, in a memo.

. . . if I ever get a speeding ticket, none of those fuckers would know me.
—Momo Salvatore "Sam" Giancana, Cosa Nostra overlord of the Chicago area, bitter at being denied access to President Kennedy. Giancana took credit for helping Kennedy win the 1960 election with strong-arm tactics.

[It's been] an unexciting and dull campaign. With me in it, it's no longer dull.
—Buz Lukens, Ohio congressman convicted of having sex with a minor, deciding to run for reelection in 1990.

I took no vow of poverty when I came to office.
—Huey "The Kingfish" Long, Louisiana governor. He petitioned the state for expensive cars and other luxury items.

No African can have an opinion that differs from mine.
—Kwame Nhrumah, 20th-century prime-minister-for-life of Ghana, who liked to be called "The Redeemer." He was deposed in a 1972 coup and died in exile.

Don't you know who runs this town?
—Rocco Pranno, boss of a crime ring centered around Chicago's O'Hare airport, to a schoolteacher who called a town meeting to protest mob-controlled city services. Pranno answered his own question by beating the teacher.

When we dropped into a polling place, everybody else dropped out.
—A member of Ragen's Colts, a Chicago-based Irish-American crime gang of the early 1920s that was named after its leader, baseball star Frank Ragen.

That man must want something: money, favors, a seat in the Supreme Court. Find out what he wants and get it for him.
—Paul "The Waiter" Ricca, Chicago Outfit mob leader, known for getting off lightly in the courts, speaking to his lawyers about the judge presiding at one of the trials against him.

Yes I do have a fair amount of money. . . . I would estimate it to total less than 50 million. What is that after 22 years as head of state of such a big country?
—Mobuto Sese Seko, president-for-life of Zaire, whose regime was called a "kleptocracy."

As long as I count the votes, what are you going to do about it?
—William "Boss" Tweed, leader of the 19th-century New York City political machine.

pontifications

Look, when we sit down to clip a guy, we have to remember what's at stake here. There's some hazard. Guys forget that. They get a guy behind in his vig payments, they get a hard-on about it, right away they want to whack him. Why? Just because they're pissed off, they're aggravated. But what I say is: "Hey, you're making a living with this guy. He gets you aggravated, and right away you want to use the hammer? How do you get your fucking money then?
—Paul Castellano, Mafia boss, to an underling.

Beauty is love made real, and the spirit of love is God. And of the state of beauty, love, and God is happiness. A transcendent state of beauty, love, and God is peace. Peace and love is a state of beauty, love, and God. One is an active state of happiness, and the other is a transcendent state. That's peace.

—Imelda Marcos, wife of the corrupt de facto dictator of the Philippines, President Ferdinand Marcos, during her husband's 1986 campaign.

Charlie made us see that once you die to your ego, once you strip yourself down to a perfect being—all body, like some monkey or a coyote free in the wild . . . fear doesn't exist anymore. You've already died. . . . You are free. Free to live, free to die. *Free to kill.*

—Tex Watson, a follower of Charles Manson, the serial killer who founded "Helter Skelter," a racist Armageddon.

possessiveness

Next time I suspect her of liking another man, I shall kill her quickly and without warning.

—Mohammed Abdullah, a.k.a. Joseph Howk, Jr., writing in his diary about his ex-girlfriend Sonja Hoff, who he shot to death on a Berkeley, California, campus.

I heard she was going to marry someone else. I was jealous of him.

—Francis "Two-Gun" Crowley, bank robber, after raping and murdering a woman.

posted

George Fresolone
THE BIGGEST MOTHERFUCKING RAT
IN NEW JERSEY AND
THE OTHER 49 STATES

—From a plaque found in an illegal gambling den, referring to Mafioso turned police informant George Fresolone.

Notice
COPS KEEP OUT!
No policeman will hereafter
be allowed on this block
By order of
THE CAR BARN GANG.
—Notice posted inside the Car Barn Gang's territory.

power

Off comes this beautiful head whenever I give the word.
—Gaius Caesar Caligula, first-century Roman emperor best known for his orgies and capricious execution orders.

It's not a toy. I'm not in the mood for toys, or games, or kidding, no time. I'm not in the mood for clans. I'm not in the mood for gangs. I'm not in the mood for none a that stuff there. And this is gonna be a Cosa Nostra till I die. Be it an hour from now, or be it tonight, or a hundred years from now when I'm in jail. It's gonna be a Cosa Nostra. . . . It's gonna be the way I say it's gonna be, and a Cosa Nostra. A "Cosa Nostra."
—John Gotti, boss of the Gambino crime family, referring to the Mafia.

preferences

I just wanted to help other people also.
—Tonya Harding, American figure skater who was convicted of plotting to injure her rival, Nancy Kerrigan, after a judge denied her request to forego the 100 hours of community service remaining on her sentence.

I'll take shooting. I'm used to that. I have been shot a few times in the past, and I guess I can stand it again.
—Joe Hill, a labor union martyr who was convicted of killing a policeman and his son as revenge for the oppression of strikers. He chose to be shot to death rather than hanged.

premonitions

From our first meeting I swore to follow you anywhere—even unto death—I live only for your love.
—Eva Braun, Adolf Hitler's mistress and wife, from a letter to the Nazi leader after the 1944 assassination attempt. Most believe they committed suicide together when it became obvious Germany had lost the war.

Me, I want to get killed in one hell-firing minute of smoking action!
—Charles Bryant, a.k.a. "Black Face Charlie," yelling to his fellow bandits after a shootout. Bryant was in fact shot to death by a deputy U.S. marshal in 1891.

I knew when I bought that first gun that it would land me in the electric chair.
—Francis "Two-Gun" Crowley, bank robber and murderer who died in the electric chair at the age of 19.

You know that "Koresh" means death. He's the rider on the pale horse.
—David Koresh, Branch Davidian cult leader who, along with his followers, burned to death when their compound caught fire during an ill-fated raid by the FBI and ATF.

My mother always said that I would die with my shoes on.
—Steve Long, professional gunman who killed many men in the 1860s, before he was hanged. His boots were removed before the noose was put around his neck.

This is serious. My head may be at stake.
—Marcel Petiot, a.k.a. Captain Henri Valéri, when the French police discovered human body parts on his property. During the Nazi occupation of France, Petiot took money from persecuted individuals and promised to help them escape, but instead poisoned and dismembered them.

press relations

How come you keep writing all those bad things about my brother Albert? He ain't killed nobody in your family . . . yet.
—Anthony Anastasio, a.k.a. "Tough Tony," waterfront racketeer, to a newspaper reporter on the subject of his brother, Mafia executioner Albert Anastasia.

It was the only way to end it all. There was no justice— so I gave it.
—Henriette Caillaux, wife of France's Minister of Finance Joseph Caillaux, on why she shot to death a Le Figaro editor after the newspaper ran several negative editorials about her husband. A jury found her innocent of murder and she was set free.

It is the absolute right of the state to supervise the formation of public opinion.
—Joseph Goebbels, Nazi propaganda minister.

THE MOST DARING TRAIN ROBBERY ON RECORD
The southbound train of the Iron Mountain railroad was stopped here this evening by five heavily armed men and robbed of __ dollars. The robbers arrived at the station a few minutes before the arrival of the train and arrested the agent and put him under guard and then threw the train on the switch. The robbers were all large men, all being slightly under six feet. After robbing the train they started in a southerly direction. They were all mounted on handsome horses.
P.S: They are a hell of an excitement in this part of the country.
—Jesse James, legendary train and bank robber of the Old West, from a statement he gave to the engineer of a train he had just robbed. James wanted his statement published in the newspapers.

You guys still with us, huh? Haven't been shot by one of my guards yet?
—David Koresh, Branch Davidian cult leader, speaking to reporters.

Ah, how I'd like to kill somebody. But it must be somebody important, so it gets in the papers.
—Luigi Luccheni, an Italian anarchist who stabbed Empress Elizabeth of Austria to death in 1898.

Who killed Lingle? Santa Claus, I'd say.
—George "Bugs" Moran, Chicago mobster, speculating on the murder of journalist Jake Lingle.

What kind of language is that to use in *The New York Times*?
—Dutch Schultz, a.k.a. Arthur Flegenheimer, New York mobster, angered that a reporter described him as a "pushover for a blonde."

prices

Ear chawed off, $15
Leg or arm broke, $19
Shot in leg, $25
Stab, $25
Doing the big job, $100 and up.
—Edward "Monk" Eastman, a.k.a. Edward Osterman, New York City crime boss of the late-19th and early-20th centuries, from his price list for services provided.

They wanted eight grand. . . . Now what do you do? I say to Pete, 50- to a 100,000 instead to get him killed. . . . Hey, that's too much money, what are you doing? I said to Arnold, let's give him 50, I'll get Pete, and Paul has to agree, okay? But I'll let [you] know, but keep your mouth shut. Don't say anything . . . because it's my ass if Tommy said 100,000 to kill a guy from Paul. . . . It may sink us all. . . . Whether it's ready or not, it's coming down . . . now play with it. That's the end of the problem.
—Tommy Gambino, mobster in the Gambino crime family, talking to the boss of the family, Paul Castellano, about a planned "hit."

Here's ten dollars, bury five of 'em.
—Michael Cassius McDonald, gambler and political fixer who installed a hand-picked puppet, Harvey Colvin, as Chicago mayor in 1874, when he was approached by two politicians asking for a two dollar contribution to help bury a deceased policeman.

Killings are cheap. They cost about $1.35 or $1.40. . . . It's like being on a quiz show. . . . When you get to ten, you go for twenty . . . you always want more.
—Stephen Nash, California drifter turned murderer.

Those cops want $300 and I can bump them off for half that much. To hell with them!
—Charles Dion O'Bannion, Chicago Northside mob boss, when told policemen wanted a payoff on bootleg liquor.

Punching	$2
Both eyes blackened	$4
Nose and jaw broke	$10
Jacked out (knocked out with a blackjack)	$15
Ear chawed off	$15
Leg or arm broke	$19
Shot in leg	$25
Stab	$25
Doing the big job [murder]	$100 and up.

—Piker Ryan, a leader of the Whyos gang active in 19th-century New York City, from a list of the gang's services found in his pocket.

Look, I want the Mick killed. He's driving me out of my
mind. I'll give a house in Winchester to any of you guys
who knocks him off.
—Dutch Schultz, a.k.a. Arthur Flegenheimer, New York mobster, complaining
about rival mobster Vincent "Mad Dog" Coll, who was disrupting Schultz's bootleg-
ging operations.

pride

Joint! You've got a nerve calling this a joint. This is an
A-number-1 house of assignation!
—Pearl "Polly" Adler, 1920s–'40s New York City madam with organized crime connections.

You don't understand. I was offered a job as a hoodlum and I turned it down cold.
—Alvin "Creepy" Karpis, freelance criminal not associated with any mob.

That night the whole place burned down at a cost of over
$100,000. Nice, eh?
—Carl Panzram, misanthropic mass murderer, after he set fire to a school warehouse.
Initially sentenced to 25 years in prison, Panzram killed again while incarcerated and
was finally executed in 1930.

I had 25 victims but they can only find nine bodies. You
under-rate me. I am Germany's greatest killer. I put
others, both here and abroad, to shame.
—Rudolf Pleil, a German man convicted of nine rape/murders, who called himself
Germany's "champion death maker."

I've got the damnedest Gestapo you ever saw.
—Artie Samash, California political lobbyist notorious for bribery, who was sentenced
to three years in prison for tax evasion, bragging to a reporter about his informants
and flunkies.

prison

I was looking at [prison] as a vacation from all the hassles.
—Shawn Eckardt, bodyguard cum "club man," who hit champion figure skater Tonya
Harding's main rival, Nancy Kerrigan, in the knee with a tire iron, in order to knock
Kerrigan out of the national figure skating championship.

privilege

Certain heads are not to be seen and you are lucky to be here.
—Hastings Kamuzu Banda, 20th-century president-for-life of Malawi.

profit

You put money into one of my companies? That was a mistake, sir. Nobody makes any money in any of my companies except me.
—Lowell McAfee Birrell, lawyer turned con man, who fooled people into investing in his companies and then bilked them dry.

Look, we've made thousands on him since he took the loan. Even if he dies tomorrow, we're way ahead.
—Frank "Funzi" Tieri, New York City-based crime boss, on a "client" of his loan shark operation.

promises

I'm the guy who's going to use this here and I'm going to make plenty of dough out of it.
—Milton Beasley, hired killer and convicted murderer turned police informer, showing off his .25 caliber automatic gun.

I'll kill him before the day is out.
—Kitty Byron, 23-year-old British woman who stabbed her lover to death, to a maid at the hotel she was thrown out of because she and her lover quarreled so loudly.

You tell this punk, I, me, John Gotti . . . will sever your motherfucking head off!
—John Gotti, boss of the Gambino crime family, on someone trying to open a gambling operation in his territory.

psychology

I knew it was me who did it but why I did it and everything else, I don't know . . . I wasn't excited. I didn't think about it. I sat down to dinner and didn't think about it at all.
—Albert Henry DeSalvo, a.k.a. "The Boston Strangler," who went home after committing murder, played with his children, ate dinner, and then watched a TV news report on the discovery of the body of one of his victims.

I did not know why I shot him. I was just very upset.
—Ruth Ellis, British nightclub manager and model, who shot her race car driver lover
to death.

[I am] afflicted with womenmania. . . . Surely they can't
punish me for enjoying lovely women . . . I go for the
57 varieties.
—Sigmund Engel, hustler who claimed to have married 200 women and conned them
out of $6 million, speaking to reporters during his trial.

Had it been 1925, it would have been 25 counts.
—Colin Ferguson, who shot 26 people on the Long Island Rail Road, killing six, claiming the reason he was indicted on 93 counts was because the crime of which he was
accused and later convicted took place in 1993.

They thought I was crazy. But I wasn't crazy. I was telling the truth.
—Momo Salvatore "Sam" Giancana, Cosa Nostra overlord of the Chicago area, referring to having been declared a "constitutional psychopath" and therefore ineligible for
the World War II draft.

I saw before me a forest of cruci-
fixes which gradually turned into
trees. At first there appeared to
be dew or rain dripping from the
branches, but as I approached I
realized it was blood. . . . A man
went to each tree catching the blood.
When the cup was full he approached
me. "Drink," he said, but I was unable to move.
—John George Haigh, a.k.a. "The Acid Bath Murderer" and "The Vampire Killer," British murderer, swindler, and forger, who immersed his victims in an acid-filled vat and then poured their liquid remains into
his backyard, recalling a frequent nightmare.

The more I looked at people, the more I hated them
because I knowed there wasn't any place for me with
the kind of people I knowed. . . . A bunch of Goddamned sons of bitches looking for somebody to make
fun of . . . .
—Charles Starkweather, mass murderer who killed his girlfriend's family and then took
her on a week-long rampage, during which he stabbed and/or shot seven people, from
his confession.

I am fairly certain that I have software I wasn't born with.
—Dennis Sweeny, a one-time volunteer for the Student Nonviolent Coordinating Committee, who shot his college mentor to death, writing in a letter to a friend.

I've been listening to that station. I wanted them to let me work there. I wrote them letters asking for work. They answered me in a song they broadcast ["There's A Ring Around The Moon"]. I recognized the message telling me to come to work every time I heard the song.
—Clarence Walter, Montana rancher who burst into the studio of radio station KHJ in Los Angeles and demanded a job, then stabbed an announcer to death.

I am prepared to die. After my death, I wish an autopsy on me to be performed to see if there is any mental disorder.
—Charles Whitman, mass murderer who shot 46 people from a bell tower at the University of Texas.

public policy

The city of necks waiting for me to chop them.
—Gaius Caesar Caligula, first-century Roman emperor.

Right is what benefits the German people, wrong is whatever harms them.
—Wilhelm Frick, Nazi minister of the interior.

Tell me, if I'm a criminal, do I still get Social Security? I haven't got a cent.
—Dolly Gee, a bank director sentenced to five years in prison on embezzlement charges.

Jersey City is the most moralest city in America.
—Frank Hague, mayor of Jersey City during the 1930s, who was supported by bookmakers and extracted a three percent kickback on the salaries of all public employees.

Whether the other peoples live in comfort or perish of hunger interests me only in so far as we need them as slaves for our Kultur.
—Heinrich Himmler, Nazi, Reichsführer-SS, head of the Gestapo and Waffen-SS, and minister of the interior of Nazi Germany, from a speech to the SS leadership.

Sounds like the skinheads did a civic duty.
—Tom Metzger, neo-Nazi and founder of the White Aryan Resistance (WAR), on the murder of an Ethiopian boy who was living in the United States.

[New York State Governor Nelson] Rockefeller did the right thing. . . . The public wants no more nonsense from criminals. The public will cheer him on. "Gun 'em down," they'll say.
—Richard Nixon, U.S. president, on New York State Governor Nelson Rockefeller's decision to send in state troopers during the 1970 riots at Attica prison, in which more than 30 inmates and nine guards died.

I desire a great and strong Germany and to achieve it I would enter an alliance with the Devil.
—Hjalmar Schacht, financial mastermind of the Third Reich and president of the Reichsbank of Nazi Germany.

A left-wing cult dedicated to bringing down the type of government I believe in.
—James G. Watt, Ronald Reagan's interior secretary, on environmentalists. Watt later pleaded guilty to a misdemeanor charge of trying to influence a federal grand jury.

public relations

. . . he worried about spending two cents for a newspaper. That was his big spending, buying the papers so's he could read about himself.
—Charles "Lucky" Luciano, mobster-founder of the national crime syndicate, speaking about fellow mobster Dutch Schultz.

. . . it was short enough to fit in the headlines. If I'd kept the name of Flegenheimer, nobody would have heard of me.
—Dutch Schultz, a.k.a. Arthur Flegenheimer, New York mobster.

I never use the words Democrats and Republicans. It's liberals and Americans.
—James G. Watt, Ronald Reagan's interior secretary, who later pleaded guilty to a misdemeanor charge of trying to influence a federal grand jury.

public service

I was helping Canada reduce its unemployment.
—Joe Bonnano, New York City Mafia boss, on "investing" in a Canadian cheese business.

Public service is my motto. Ninety-nine percent of the people in Chicago drink and gamble. I've tried to serve them decent liquor and square games. But I'm not appreciated. It's no use. I violate the prohibition law, sure. Who doesn't? The only difference is I take more chance than the man who drinks a cocktail before dinner and a flock of highballs after it. But he's just as much violator as I am.
—Al Capone, legendary mobster who controlled Chicago during the 1920s and '30s, on his activities during Prohibition.

I talk about my experience and the need to get their lives together, the need to recognize mistakes were made but they aren't a bad person.
—Sol Wachtler, New York State Supreme Court justice who pleaded guilty to threatening to kidnap his mistress's 14-year-old daughter, on what he says in self esteem lectures he gives to youths.

punishment

Death by torture.
—Edmund Emil Kemper III, a California man who murdered, and in some cases dismembered, eight people, when asked what he thought would be an appropriate punishment for his crimes.

quality

We competed by having the best powder because drug addicts don't buy names, they buy quality.
—Nicky Barnes, Harlem drug lord with Mafia ties.

We left the bum under a billboard that says, "Drive Safely." Lucky was satisfied plenty.
—Abe Reles, a paid killer for Murder, Inc., describing the murder of a kidnapping victim, done for the crime boss "Lucky" Luciano in 1934.

quantity

The more the merrier.
John Reginald Halliday Christie, Londoner who killed at least six women, in a statement in which he confessed to the murder of a woman for which another man had been hanged

It might have been 30. It might have been 40. I don't remember.

—Fritz Haarman, a.k.a. "The Ogre of Hanover," German mass murderer who preyed on young men by kidnapping, molesting, butchering, and eating them, sometimes even selling their flesh as food in the market, trying to recall how many he had killed.

(good) questions

After my head has been chopped off, will I still be able to hear at least for a moment the sound of my own blood gushing from the stump of my neck? That would be the pleasure to end all pleasures.

—Peter Kürten, a.k.a. "The Düsseldorf Vampire," who drank the blood of some of his nine murder victims and sexually assaulted at least 23 other people, speaking to his executioner a moment before he was beheaded in 1931.

Have you ever thought that you may die for the Unification Church? . . . Will you complain against me at the moment of death?

—Rev. Sun Myung Moon, cult leader and newspaper publisher known for officiating at mass marriages and for tax evasion.

. . . I been meaning to ask you. That time when I cooked some of those people. Why'd I do that?

—Ottis Toole, an arsonist and serial killer, speaking to his partner, Henry Lee Lucas, in a telephone conversation taped by the police. Together, Toole and Lucas are believed to have murdered 108 people.

Is this all there is to it?

—Dr. Arthur Warren Waite, New York dentist who killed his in-laws in an attempt to inherit their estate, as he took his place in the electric chair at Sing Sing prison in 1917.

quid pro quo

I've done you a good turn. Now you do one for me. Will you kill me?

—William Nelson Adams, a 17-year-old who was given food and lodging by a 60-year-old man he later stabbed nearly to death. Adams claimed that the older man asked him to kill him by saying the above. A jury found Adams not credible and the judge sentenced him to death; his sentence was later commuted to life imprisonment.

When I became a criminal, it was obvious I wasn't going to live long. Everyone around me was dying. I witnessed a murder and I knew my life had ended. . . .
—Billie Beattie, Westies gang member.

I hunted because I was hunted myself, and I showed no consideration for anybody or anything because I knew I would receive none.
—Jack Black, professional burglar from 1870 to 1900 who eventually went straight, ending up as a reporter for a newspaper.

Nobody puts a price on my head and lives.
—Al Capone, a.k.a. "Scarface," legendary mobster who controlled Chicago during the 1920s and '30s.

I hate everybody's guts and they hate mine.
—William Cook, early 1950s robber and murderer.

It is by the heart that you made me suffer and it is by the heart that you will die!
—Marin Fenayrou, a French druggist, recounting what he said to his wife's lover as he stabbed him in the chest, killing him.

What did she step on my heart for?
—Vito Genovese, head of the Genovese crime family, responding to damning testimony from his battered wife who arrived in court with two black eyes.

Well, it's my turn to be put in the sack now.
—Vasili Komaroff, a.k.a. "The Wolf of Moscow," a mass murderer responsible for at least 30 deaths, after he was sentenced to be shot in 1923.

Society will have my blood, but I in my turn shall have the blood of society.
—Pierre François Laçenaire, a would be-poet, lamenting his plight after confessing to two murders.

I'm a criminal! I murdered someone! I owe society a life!
—Gertrude Morris, who shot her husband to death because she was jealous of the attention he paid to his secretary, shouting to reporters in the courtroom at her trial. Apparently Morris was hoping to get the death penalty.

If I live I'll execute some more of you!
—Carl Panzram, misanthropic mass murderer, after a judge sentenced him to 25 years in prison. Panzram killed again while incarcerated and was executed in 1930.

Visit me!

—Carl Panzram, misanthropic mass murderer, shouting to the judge after being sentenced to 25 years in prison. Panzram killed again while incarcerated and was executed in 1930.

My only desire is to reform people who try to reform me. And I believe that the only way to reform people is to kill 'em.

—Carl Panzram, misanthropic mass murderer, after a judge sentenced him to 25 years in prison. Panzram killed again while incarcerated and was executed in 1930.

I had hated and been hated. I had my little world to keep alive as long as possible, and my gun. That was my answer.

—Charles Starkweather, mass murderer who killed his girlfriend's family and then took her on a week-long rampage, during which he stabbed and/or shot seven people, from his confession.

rationalizations

I never killed a man who didn't need it.

—Robert A. Allison, Confederate Army soldier, cowboy, and murderer of an estimated 15 men.

You're here to help me, and by helping me you're going to help a lot of people.

—Jim Bakker, TV evangelist, seducing church secretary Jessica Hahn. Hahn later appeared in *Playboy*, and Bakker later went to jail, convicted of 24 counts of mail and wire fraud.

I have killed no man that in the first place didn't deserve killing by the standards of our way of life.

—Mickey Cohen, California gangster who started as Bugsy Siegel's bodyguard.

I lost my innocence at age eight so I decided to do the same to as many young girls as I could.

—Pedro Alonzo Lopez, Colombian man who claims to have raped and murdered more than 200 girls.

reasoning

I'd cheat people if it would make me one more dollar, but it won't.

—Benny Binion, Nevada gambling king.

redundancies

I'm not deaf, I just don't hear so good.

—Frank Abbandando, a.k.a "The Dasher," hit man for Murder, Inc., claiming he could not hear the long list of crimes that the prosecution was itemizing during his 1940 trial, at which Abbandando was sentenced to death in the electric chair.

regrets

I tip more than that. Why'd I kill a bum for a lousy 80 bucks?

—Louis "Pretty" Amberg, mobster believed to have killed over 100 people, brushing off a murder he was suspected of having committed.

Funny thing, I've always got such fun out of life. I liked to live and spend money. Maybe I made it in ways some folks call crooked, but I always worked hard, whatever I went at. Life is awfully sweet. You never know how much you want to live until you come to a fix like this. I shot men in my time but I never shot one who didn't deserve it.

—Charles Birger, bootlegger and killer, speaking on the morning he was hanged.

Just one more would have made an even number.

—Sydney Jones, mass murderer who killed 13 men, from a note found in his jail cell after he was hanged.

In the old days, before the revolution, the Mafiya really worked for the people. There was a group that once kidnapped Lenin. But they didn't believe it was really him, and they let him go. They should have shot the bastard then—we would never have had the Communist nightmare.

—Ted Kasyanov, Russian strongman arrested in Russia for murder and kidnapping.

If I had had my .44, I would have caught him.

—Sara Jane Moore, a police and FBI informant who attempted to shoot President Gerald Ford with a .38 caliber handgun in 1975. The .44 caliber gun had been confiscated just one day earlier by the police.

There goes 15 years down the drain.

Arizona restaurateur Steven Steinberg, who killed his wife by stabbing her 26 times.

relativity

Better that ten thousand others die than he be lost
to Germany.
—Eva Braun, Adolf Hitler's mistress and wife, talking about the Nazi leader.

In the 1960s and 1970s, there were
many student movements and turmoils
in the United States. Did they have
any other recourse but to mobilize
police and troops, arrest people, and
shed blood?
—Deng Xiaoping, Chinese leader, after the massacre at Tiananmen Square in 1989.

That's really cruel. I wonder what would cause a man to
do such a thing.
—Sirhan Bishara Sirhan, Palestinian assassin of Senator Robert F. Kennedy, wondering why
"The Boston Strangler" made elaborate bows out of the stockings he used to strangle his
victims. Sirhan was under arrest and talking to a police sergeant at the time.

relax

Don't get excited! It didn't go off. It didn't go off!
—Lynette "Squeaky" Fromme, a member of Charles Manson's cult of killers, after the
pistol she trained on President Gerald Ford didn't fire.

relief

Oh, God, for a minute I thought you were a policeman!
—George Shotton, an Englishman posthumously convicted of murdering an ex-cho-
rus girl in Wales, England, remarking to the mailman while carrying a sack containing
the girl's corpse. Shotton died before the body was discovered.

requests

Have someone play a fiddle when I swing off.
—"Black Jack" Ketchum, outlaw train robber of the Old West to the warden on the day
Ketchum was to hang. An incorrectly tied rope caused Ketchum's head to be ripped from
his body when the trap door opened.

Will you die for me, Tex? Will you let me kill you? . . .
Let me kill you.
—Charles Manson, mass murderer and leader of "Helter Skelter," a racist Armaged-
don, to one of his followers.

respect

It's funny how some people get respect. . . . I got my
respect by fucking them up.
—Mike Tyson, heavyweight champion boxer convicted of rape, on his childhood life
of crime.

retirement

Well tell the folks I'm going away now. I guess murder
will stop. There won't be anymore booze. You won't be
able to find a crap game. . . .
—Al Capone, a.k.a. "Scarface," legendary mobster who controlled Chicago during the
1920s and '30s, before retiring to Florida.

retribution

If you want to be a little Jesus Christ, then we'll make one out of you.
—Anonymous thugs "Swede" and "Joe," speaking to Ed Collins, a robber who had recently been re-
leased from prison and refused to help them plan a robbery. They spoke the above after they had nailed
Collins to a homemade cross.

I'm going to kill that guy as soon as I can hold a gun!
—Fred Barker, murderer, bank robber, and son of the infamous Ma Barker, speaking
about the black-market doctor, Joseph Moran, who botched the plastic surgery on Fred
Barker's face and fingertips that was supposed to conceal his identity.

I expect no favor from the hands of a jailor, who comes
of the race of those angels that fell with Lucifer from
Heaven, whither you'll never return again. Of all your
bunches of keys not one hath wards to open that door;
for a jailor's soul stands not upon those two pillars that
support Heaven, Justice, and Mercy; it rather sits upon
those two footstools of Hell, Wrong, and Cruelty. So
make no more words about your purse, for have it I will,
or else your life.
—Richard Dudley, 17th-century British murderer and robber, to his former jailer whom
he subsequently robbed.

Well they haven't done anything to me yet. But I am doing plenty to them.
—Howard Unruh, army sharpshooter who shot 13 people to death in a 12-minute rampage in Camden, New Jersey, in 1949, when asked whether the police, who had surrounded the house in which he had barricaded himself, had harmed him.

revenge

You dirty rat! You started this. We'll end it. You're as good as dead!
—Louis Campagna, Al Capone's bodyguard, to rival mobster Joseph Aiello, after Aiello offered to flee Chicago when his plot to overthrow Capone failed.

I am spending your money to have you and your family killed—nice, eh?
—George "Machine Gun" Kelly, bank robber and kidnapper of the 1920s and '30s, from a letter he wrote to his kidnapping victim, Charles F. Urschel, after he had received the ransom money and released Urschel. Kelly was angry because his in-laws had been arrested; he held Urschel responsible. Urschel's family was not harmed.

Senator, I got the score. The score was, we lost 1 and they lost from 40 to 60.
—Joseph Valachi, a henchman in the Genovese crime family, on how vengeance was exacted among crime families, in testimony given during Senate sub-committee hearings in 1964.

rewards

I got him—can I have a cigarette?
—Louis Cohen, a.k.a. Louis Kushner, a novice underling to the infamous Jake "Legs" Diamond, confessing to the police after killing a rival gangster.

rhetorical questions

Arthur, why don't you put a gun in your mouth and see how many times you can pull the trigger?
—Louis "Pretty" Amberg, mobster believed to have killed over 100 people, to mobster Dutch Schultz, when Schultz suggested that he wanted to move into Amberg's numbers racket in Brooklyn. Arthur was Schultz's real name.

Well, I got out, didn't I?
—J. Harvey Bailey, bank robber during the "golden age" of Dillinger, Bonnie and Clyde, and others, when asked what he thought he would prove by escaping from prison.

If I'm such a bad criminal, why am I still walking around free?
—Francesco Cotroni, a.k.a "Santos," "Frank," and the "Big Guy," mobster who controlled the Canadian branch of Joe Bonnano's Mafia operation. Cotroni was eventually imprisoned for loan sharking, extortion, counterfeiting, and distributing narcotics and pornography.

Do we have to shed blood to reform the current political system? I hope it doesn't come to that. But it might.
—Timothy J. McVeigh, former army sergeant accused of bombing the Murrah federal office building in Oklahoma City, Oklahoma.

rites of passage

This thing has to be done. . . . it's business, and I want you to be the shooter so you'll have this behind you.
—Pasquale Martirano, a.k.a. Patty Specs, underboss of the Bruno/Scarfo crime family, giving the order to carry out a murder. Before becoming a "made" member of the Mafia it was a necessary rite of passage to carry out a "hit."

. . . this is the most important day in your life. Today you become one of us. It's long over-due. I'm happy I can do this for you.
—Anthony Piccolo, a.k.a. "Tony Buck" and "Cousin Anthony," consigliere to the Bruno/Scarfo crime family, after the ceremony that inducted a new member, George Fresolone, to the family. Fresolone had already turned police informant and was wired with a listening device at the time.

rivals and rivalry

This is silly. If it's money you want, you can have it, but don't try this gun stuff.
—George "Big Frenchy" DeMange, bootlegger and gambling operator of the 1920s and '30's, speaking to mobster Vincent Coll, who was holding him hostage.

They're punks—they're giving bank-robbing a bad name.
—John Dillinger, infamous bank robber of the 1920s and '30s, upon reading of the robberies committed by Bonnie and Clyde.

They were all done by that dirty atheistic dago!
—Charles Dion O'Bannion, Chicago Northside mob boss, rival of Al Capone.

I know where I am. I've been here before. I just came to tell you that I'll pay good to any cop who kills the Mick!
—Dutch Schultz, a.k.a. Arthur Flegenheimer, New York mobster, at a police station, asking the police if they would kill his rival gangster Vincent "Mad Dog" Coll.

We have to get rid of these people.
—Joseph Valachi, a henchman in the Genovese crime family, paraphrasing boss mobster Salvatore Maranzano, who was talking about rival mobsters such as Al Capone and Frank Costello.

romance

Well, that one doesn't count really—I married the girl later.
—Frank Abbandando, a.k.a "The Dasher," hit man for Murder, Inc., when asked about his sexual attack on a woman.

My story is a love story. But only those tortured by love can know what I mean. I am not unfeeling, stupid or moronic. I am a woman who had a great love and always will have it. . . .
—Martha Beck, registered nurse who swindled and murdered as many as 23 people, writing about her love affair with her con artist boyfriend and partner in crime, Raymond Fernandez, while she sat on death row.

. . . Joe Colombo's father was fooling around with a member of organized-crime's girlfriend or wife and they caught them in a car together. The next day when the cops found them they were both dead, shot in the head. But the unfortunate thing is that they cut off his prick and stuck it in his own mouth.
—Joseph "Joey" Cantalupo, Colombo crime family associate.

I was searching for the perfect mate, the real romance of life.
—Nannie Doss, Oklahoma woman who murdered 11 people, including four of her five husbands.

People want to know whether I still love Martha. But of course I do. I want to shout it out. I love Martha. What do the public know about love?
—Raymond Martinez Fernandez, a.k.a. Charles Martin, a killer who found his victims in the lonely hearts column of the newspaper, from the note he wrote just before dying in the electric chair. He was married to Martha Julie Beck—together they were known as the "Lonely Hearts Killers"—and admitted to killing 17 people in order to rob them of their savings.

Joey made me feel like a woman.

—Amy Fisher, a.k.a. "The Long Island Lolita," who shot the wife of her married lover, Joey Buttafuoco, in the head. Buttafuoco was convicted of statutory rape in the case, and, according to Fisher, he turned Fisher into a prostitute, compelled her to use diet medicine to get her weight down to 80 pounds, and encouraged her to try to kill his wife.

Triflers need not apply.

—Belle Gunness, Indiana farm woman who advertised in newspapers for marriage-minded men. The ads concluded with the above caveat. After luring men to her farm, she then drugged, robbed, murdered, butchered, and buried them, killing 14 in all. She was acquitted of murdering her first husband, who was found bludgeoned to death, even though one of her children would skip through the streets of La Porte singing, "Momma killed Daddy with a hatchet!"

His name wasn't Bugsy Siegel, it was Ben, Ben Siegel! And he was no gangster—what do you know? Why, that man loved poetry! There was a poem both of us kept— Aww, you jerks wouldn't understand.

—Virginia Hill, mob "bagman" (money carrier) and girlfriend of mobster Bugsy Siegel, to reporters, after the death of Siegel.

Jodie, I would abandon this idea of getting Reagan in a second if I could only win your heart and live out the rest of my life with you, whether it be in total obscurity or whatever. I will admit to you that the reason I'm going ahead with this attempt now is because I just cannot wait any longer to impress you. I've got to do something now to make you understand in no uncertain terms that I am doing all this for your sake. By sacrificing my freedom and possibly my life, I hope to change your mind about me.

—John W. Hinckley, the Colorado man who shot President Ronald Reagan in an effort to win the affections of actress Jodie Foster. Hinckley shot Reagan after seeing Foster in the movie *Taxi Driver*, in which a gunman attempts a political assassination.

Wishes acquaintance of widow . . . object matrimony.

—Johann Hoch, a Chicago man who married as many as three times per year, then poisoned his wives and took their money, from an advertisement he ran in a newspaper.

One side of me says, "Wow, what an attractive chick, I'd like to talk to her, date her." The other side of me says, "I wonder how her head would look on a stick."

—Edmund Emil Kemper III, a California man who murdered eight people.

I want to kill a girl. . . . I think I can get away with it.
—Charles Howard Schmid, murderer who lured a 15-year-old girl to the desert and killed her.

He wanted to marry me or elope with me. I tried to pacify him by pretending that I was poisoning my husband.
—Jeanne Daniloff Weiss, a French woman who conspired with her lover to poison her husband in 1890.

savings/economies
What a great saving.
—Augusto Pinochet, ruthless Chilean dictator, when he heard that victims of his coup were buried two to a coffin.

science

"[Science] will conquer famine, eliminate psychological suffering, make everybody healthy and happy." Yeah, sure.
—Unabomber, anonymous terrorist—believed to be Theodore Kaczynski—who sent bombs through the mail, causing three deaths and numerous injuries, from his manifesto published jointly by *The New York Times* and *Washington Post.*

self-improvement

Remember the three R's:
Respect for self
Respect for others
Responsibility for all your actions.
—Aldrich Ames, CIA agent secretly working for the KGB, wrote three checks at the bottom of this page from his calendar.

self-knowledge

I was never rich, but I was important.
—Tommaso Buscetta, Sicilian Mafia leader now in the federal witness protection program, on his life in organized crime.

Sometimes lust takes over me. It's very painful.
—Joey Buttafuoco, Long Island mechanic turned tabloid T.V. regular, who was convicted of statutory rape, pled no contest to the charge of attempting to solicit a prostitute, and was accused of encouraging his underage girlfriend, Amy Fisher, "The Long Island Lolita," to shoot his wife.

If I was the government, I'd put my ass in jail for a thousand years.
—Paul Castellano, a.k.a. "Big Paul," Mafia boss of the Gambino family.

All I know I stole. If I saw you hold a cigarette in a certain way, and I liked it, I would steal it from you.
—Frank Costello, Mafia boss.

I'm no saint, but I swear to you that I'm no bum either.
—Francesco Cotroni, a.k.a "Santos," "Frank," and the "Big Guy," mobster who controlled the Canadian branch of Joe Bonnano's Mafia operation. Cotroni was imprisoned for loan sharking, extortion, counterfeiting, and distributing narcotics and pornography.

I'm a hoodlum. I don't want to be a legitimate guy. All these other racket guys who get a few bucks want to become legitimate.
—Angelo "Gyp" DeCarlo, New Jersey-based Mafia boss.

I entered a mail car at Phoenix, Arizona, with intentions to rob. The mail clerk refused to submit to robbery, and, although unarmed, he attacked me and I was forced to either surrender to him or shoot him. That mail clerk was a 100 percent man and I was a cheap crook. The result was inevitable.
—Roy Gardner, train robber and escape artist dubbed Public Enemy Number One, recalling one of the crimes that put him in jail.

You can't do nothing to me. I'm sick.
—Arthur Frederick Goode III, infamous child molester and murderer, speaking to the police upon his arrest for the murder of an 11-year-old boy.

I was proud to be Nixon's son-of-a-bitch.
—Robert Haldeman, member of President Nixon's cabinet.

I am the worst man who ever lived!
—Albert E. Hicks, 19th-century pirate and murderer, to one of his jailers on the morning of his hanging

We are a race of savages and have no pity.
—Adolf Hitler, Nazi leader.

I am devoted to fire. Fire is my master. . . .
—Bruce Lee, British pyromaniac who was responsible for the deaths of 26 people.

I get nasty.
—Wendell Willis Lightbourne, a Bermuda teenager who murdered three women while working as a golf caddy, during his confession to the police.

There's no reason denying what we become. We know what we are.
—Henry Lee Lucas, mass murderer, speaking to his partner in many of his 90 killings, Ottis Toole, in a conversation wiretapped by the police. Toole was known to have eaten some of the victims.

Life with me is just one bullet after another.
—Edward "Spike" O'Donnell, leader of a gang of bootleggers in Prohibition-era Chicago. O'Donnell was frequently the target of rival gangsters.

I was the spirit of meanness personified.
—Carl Panzram, misanthropic mass murderer, after being court-martialed and serving three years in prison at hard labor. Later, after committing more crimes, Panzram was sentenced to 25 years in prison, but he killed again while incarcerated and was executed in 1930.

I am nursing a viper in Rome's bosom.
—Tiberius, perverted and blood-thirsty Emperor of Rome from 14 B.C. to A.D. 37, on his nephew and chosen successor, the even more severely debauched Caligula.

I always had a very ungovernable temper.
—Elizabeth Van Valkenburgh, 19th-century New York State woman who poisoned her two husbands with arsenic.

self-pity

I've been spending the best years of my life as a public benefactor. I've given the people the light pleasures, shown them a good time. And all I get is abuse—the existence of a hunted man—I'm called a killer.
—Al Capone, a.k.a. "Scarface," legendary mobster who controlled Chicago and its politics during the 1920s and '30s, referring to his gambling and liquor operations during Prohibition.

Whadda ya mean, 'surrounded by violence'? People are shooting at me.
—Mickey Cohen, California gangster who started out as Bugsy Siegel's bodyguard, responding to the following question, put to him by Senator Charles Tobey at the Kefauver committee's hearings on organized crime in 1950: "Is it not a fact that you live extravagantly . . . surrounded by violence?"

It's no fun having to spend all your evenings and week-
ends preparing dangerous mixtures, filing trigger mecha-
nism out of scraps of metal or searching the [S]ierras for
a place isolated enough to test a bomb.
—Unabomber, anonymous terrorist—believed to Theodore Kaczynski—who sent bombs
through the mail, causing three deaths and numerous injuries.

sex

This runs totally counter to my dignity.
—Tommaso Buscetta, Sicilian Mafia leader, when accused of using a prison infirmary to have sex with
his visiting girlfriend.

He slept with every woman he could and I've had it!
—Jean Harris, the school headmistress who murdered her lover, Herman Tarnower, the
Scarsdale Diet Doctor.

She wanted to marry me, but it was not for a home or
for children, but to have someone like me at her disposal.
She thought of nothing else. . . . I didn't want to marry a
loving machine.
—Jean Liger, a Frenchman who murdered his lover, from a statement in court.

So when I wanted to get some, I used to turn to Gay
Orlova or Polly Adler.
—Charles "Lucky" Luciano, top crime boss of the 1920s, who claimed he was merely
a customer of the two madams, Orlova and Adler. In reality, Luciano ran an empire of
prostitution, and was later imprisoned on dozens of prostitution-related crimes.

Did I win the Lotto?
—Mel Reynolds, Illinois congressman, upon hearing an 18-year-old woman suggest
a "threesome" with a 15-year-old girl.

sharing

What the fuck! . . . Well, here's how it seems to me. If
it's thirds, it's thirds and cut the bull shit excuses. Look,
we got a third of the jobs, and I want a third of the
money. A third of the jobs and a third of the responsibility. I want a third of everything, get it? It's rightfully mine
and I want it.
—Paul Castellano, a.k.a. "Big Paul," Mafia boss in the Gambino family, speaking about
how the garment district spoils should be divided.

short answers

The KGB.
—Aldrich Ames, CIA agent secretly working for the KGB, responding to the question, "For whom would you rather work, the CIA or the KGB, if you could live your life over again?"

Killing mice.
—Mary Eleanor Pearcey, Briton who slashed another woman to death, when asked by the police what she had been doing in her house to cause the numerous bloodstains they found.

There isn't any.
—Vincent Teresa, confessed Mafia member, when asked where the term "honor among thieves" came from.

skills

We've added another round to our bag of tricks . . . murder.
—Harold Walter Bean, who murdered an 81-year-old widow in order to receive an insurance payoff, speaking to a friend.

slogans

The white revolution is the only solution.
—Tom Metzger, neo-Nazi and founder of the White Aryan Resistance (WAR).

My motto is: 'Rob 'em all, rape'em all and kill 'em all!'
—Carl Panzram, misanthropic mass murderer. Initially sentenced to 25 years in prison, Pazram killed again while incarcerated and was executed in 1930.

Victory or Death
—World War II Fascist Party slogan.

society

Being an uneducated person, what walk of life could I have gotten into that I could have become involved with such people? . . . I'm talking about celebrities, politicians, people in higher walks of life and education and different things like that.
—Mickey Cohen, mobster.

sports

No, we really weren't into that.
—Aldrich Ames, CIA agent secretly working for the KGB, when asked if he and his
father talked about football.

To be perfectly honest, what I'm thinking about are dollar signs.
—Tonya Harding, U.S. figure skater, upon winning the 1994 national championship. She
was later convicted of participating in the plot to club her main competitor, Nancy
Kerrigan, in the knee, which left Kerrigan unable to compete for the national title.

Jack and I were going out to play a little golf.
—Sam "Golf Bag" Hunt, hit man for Al Capone and Murder, Inc., who was known for carrying a shotgun
in his golf bag, to a police detective who was searching Hunt's bag after a passerby heard a shot fired
on the golf course.

There's no hunting in the world like hunting men.
—Will Irwin, early-20th-century con man.

I am a lover of outdoor sports.
—George "Bugs" Moran, Chicago mobster of the 1920s and '30s, explaining his love
of shotguns.

spouses

My wife has accomodated [sic] herself to what I am doing in a very supportive way.
—Aldrich Ames, CIA agent secretly working for the KGB, in a note regarding his wife
and her knowledge that he was spying for the Soviets and taking millions of dollars in
payment for doing so.

I could take her and crush her.
—Adolph Luetgert, German immigrant sausage-maker whose wife's remains were found
at the bottom of a vat in his factory. He was speaking about his wife and being quoted
by one of his mistresses at his murder trial.

stoicism

We took the guy out in the woods, and I said, "Now listen. . . . You gotta go. Why not let me hit you right in the heart, and you won't feel a thing?" He said, "I'm innocent . . . but if you've gotta do it . . . . " So I hit him in the heart, and it went right through him.
—Angelo "Gyp" DeCarlo, New Jersey-based Mafia boss, reminiscing about a "hit."

No man will stand it better than I.
—William E. Delaney, a.k.a. "Mormon Bill," an outlaw of the Old West, boasting that he didn't fear his impending hanging.

Most of you know what it means to see a hundred corpses lying together, 500, or 1,000. To have stuck it out and at the same time—apart from exceptions caused by human weakness—to have remained decent fellows, that is what has made us hard.
—Heinrich Himmler, Nazi, Reichsführer-SS, head of the Gestapo and Waffen-SS, and minister of the interior of Nazi Germany, from a speech to the SS leadership.

I don't care whether you sentence me to death or not!
—George J. Smith, British man who killed the three women he married in order to cash in their life insurance policies, shouting to the court after the prosecution finished presenting its case. He was hanged in 1915.

strategy

I act stupid.
—Francesco Cotroni, a.k.a "Santos," "Frank," and the "Big Guy," mobster who controlled the Canadian branch of Joe Bonnano's Mafia operation, on how he deals with the police.

What I think is that we're a bunch of saps if we turn this son-of-a-bitch loose! Kill the bastard! Then we won't have any more trouble with him!
—Kathryn Thorne Kelly, kidnapper and wife of George "Machine Gun" Kelly, talking about their kidnap victim, millionaire oil magnate Charles F. Urschel. Kathryn Kelly had masterminded the kidnapping plot and her husband's public image.

Is every smoking chimney and every bad smell proof that a body is being burned?
—Henri Desire Landru, a.k.a. "Bluebeard," the French mass murderer who, according to conservative estimates, killed 20 women, responding at his trial to the evidence that his neighbors complained of a stench wafting out of his chimney. Landru cut up the bodies into small pieces and burned them in his home.

The boxes were marked "poison." That was all I needed to know.
—Christa Ambros Lehmann, German housewife and murderer who claimed she only intended to make her friend sick with poisoned chocolates, but ended up killing her instead.

If it don't work, you go to the slammer, which I imagine would take up most of my future.
—James McDougal, business partner of President Bill Clinton and owner of the savings and loan association that issued bad loans and was involved in the Whitewater real estate scandal, explaining that his defense rested on President Clinton's testimony.

. . . we would wine and dine and when they were drunk enough they would go to bed. When they were asleep I would get my .45 Colt Army Automatic . . . and blow their brains out.
—Carl Panzram, misanthropic mass murderer, describing how he lured sailors to his yacht and then killed them. Initially sentenced to 25 years in prison, Panzram killed again while incarcerated and was executed in 1930.

You know what I'll do. I'll get a knife, I'll cut out his tongue, and we'll send it to his wife. We put it in an envelope, put a stamp on it.
—John Stanfa, Philadelphia mob boss convicted of racketeering charges, including conspiring to commit murder and heading a ring that engaged in kidnapping and gambling.

style

I think only queers wear silk shirts. I never bought one in my life. A guy's a sucker to spend $15 or $20 a shirt. Hell, a guy can get a good one for two bucks!
—Dutch Schultz, a.k.a. Arthur Flegenheimer, New York mobster, on style.

suggestions

Of course I know I am done for and when you kill me I suggest you have my head mounted and hang it up in the courthouse for the sake of law and order.
—Carl Durand, expert outdoorsman and the son of a Wyoming rancher, who killed five men after shooting game out of season. Durand ultimately killed himself during a failed bank holdup.

surprise

Oh no! How did she die?
—Robert Chambers, a.k.a. "The Preppie Murderer," upon being told that the young woman he strangled was dead.

Well, you see him now!
—John Wesley Hardin, possibly the fastest and most feared gunman of the Old West, to two Union soldiers, one of whom had just asked Hardin, "Do you know what he [Hardin] looks like?" To punctuate his answer Hardin pulled out his six-guns, killing one soldier and wounding the other.

I hate to tell you this but I've been robbing banks for a year and a half.
—William Liebscher, Jr., a Florida car salesman who moonlighted as a bank robber, speaking to his wife after his arrest.

What—is there anything left to be buried?
—Frederick Small, who murdered his wife with a poker and then set fire to their house, expressing surprise when the coroner asked him what he wanted done with the body.

We dug him up after he died, and his hair was still growing. The dead man was hairy. I never saw this before.
—"Tony," anonymous Mafia hit man, discussing digging up the body of one of his victims.

taunts

Catch me if you can
—Tom Bell, surgeon turned stagecoach robber, from a note to the posse of lawmen on his trail. The posse eventually caught up with Bell and hanged him.

You'll never get me. I'll kill again. Then you'll have another long trial. And I'll do it again.
—Henry Brisbon, Jr., a.k.a. "The I-57 Killer," who was convicted of two counts of murder and conspiring to commit murder. In prison, Brisbon attempted to murder two inmates.

You dirty fish-peddling bums! Leave this innocent girl alone and get the right one which is nobody else but us! . . . We defy you to catch us!
—Cecelia Cooney, a.k.a. "The Bobbed-Haired Bandit," in a message to the police after they arrested the wrong woman.

Your turn comes on Friday, so think about it.
—Irma Grese, Nazi concentration camp supervisor, to an inmate, after having just killed another inmate.

Mrs. Durand-Deacon no longer exists! I've destroyed her with acid. . . . You can't prove murder without a body.
—John George Haigh, a.k.a. "The Acid Bath Murderer" and "The Vampire Killer," British swindler and forger who immersed his victims in an acid-filled vat and then poured their liquid remains into his backyard.

I see you are still having no luck catching me. . . . I reckon your boys are letting you down. . . . You can't be much good, can ya? . . . Well, I'll keep on going for quite a while yet. Even if you do get near I'll probably top myself first. Well it's been nice chatting to you, . . . Yours, Jack the Ripper.
—Peter William Sutcliffe, a.k.a. "The Yorkshire Ripper," British serial killer, from a tape sent to the police.

teamwork

Until the Commission meets and puts its foot down things will be at a standstill. When we meet, we all got to shake hands, and sit down and talk, and, if there is any trouble with a regime, it's got to be kept secret.
—Michelino Clemente, Profaci crime family member.

territory

The first thing you'll see in my area is this gun. . . . And it'll be the last thing you see.
—Louis "Pretty" Amberg, mobster, warning rival mobster Dutch Schultz not to move into his territory.

This is the safest territory in the world for a big meet. We could've scattered you guys in my motels; we could've given you different cars from my auto agencies, and then we could've had the meet in one of my big restaurants. The cops don't bother us there. We got three towns just outside of Chicago with the police chiefs in our pocket. We got what none of you guys got. We got this territory locked up tight.
—Momo Salvatore "Sam" Giancana, Cosa Nostra overlord of the Chicago area, to a fellow mobster from Buffalo.

therapy

[The counselor] has helped me see the truth of my inappropriate and wrong response to the situation in which I found myself. [She] has also helped me acknowledge the pain, abuse and powerlessness I have felt during the years I have worked as a laywoman on a senior level at the church headquarters.
—Ellen F. Cooke, who earned $125,000 as treasurer of the national Episcopal church, on why she stole $2.2 million from the church and used the money to buy homes, jewelry, and limousine rides.

You mean I killed my mother instead of Betty Gore?
—Candy Montgomery, speaking to her therapist, who hypothesized that Candy killed her lover's wife with 41 ax blows because Candy's mother had stifled Candy's childhood rage. Candy was acquitted of murder.

threats

You know, we got a lot of laundry bags at the shop. You don't sign up with us, you're gonna be in one of them bags.
—Louis "Pretty" Amberg, mobster, issuing his standard threat to anyone who didn't use his laundry service.

If we are going to start a war, it will be with the United States.
—Shoko Asahara, leader of the Japanese cult Aum Shinrikyo (Supreme Truth), in a videotaped statement made while he was in hiding after masterminding poison gas attacks in the Tokyo subway system.

Shaddup or I'll bust ya in da teets [teeth].
—Sam Battaglia, a.k.a. "Teets," loan shark who worked for Al Capone, speaking the words for which he was famous and for which he was given the name "Teets."

I've been persecuted something awful and I'm liable to kill somebody anytime.
—James E. Bell, who killed two people in a paranoid fit before killing himself in 1929.

If it comes down to it, me and you, you'll see heaven before I do.
—Tommy Bilotti, bodyguard to mobster Paul Castellano, talking to a detective.

I'm not going to be a single parent. . . . He'll die first.
—Betty Broderick, California homemaker, referring to her ex-husband, who she shot
and killed along with his new wife.

Then we know what we gotta do then, we, we, go and roll it up and go to war. I don't know if that's what you want.
—Aniello Dellacroce, underboss in the Gambino crime family, threatening a fellow mobster.

[Engrave it,] "From Sam to Bob," so that when they find
you in a trunk they'll know I was your friend.
—Sam DeStefano, Chicago Outfit hit man and renowned sadist, to a man who owed
money to a loan shark. He took the man to a jeweler, bought him a watch, and had
it engraved.

When I get out I'll make Carlo Gambino shit in the middle
of Times Square.
—Carmine Galante, a.k.a. "Mr. Lilo," mobster in the Bonnano crime family, on rival
Mafioso Carlo Gambino.

I know what's goin' on. . . . You're oblivious to what's
goin' on, but I ain't. I'm in the fuckin' hunt. . . . Me, I'll
always be all right.
—John Gotti, boss of the Gambino crime family, who was eventually sent to jail.

You're mad to think you can keep me in here. I'll get
loose again some day and then I'll kill. Do you understand? Kill!
—Daniel Paul Harrison, murderer of five people, speaking to a guard at the hospital
for the criminally insane in which he was incarcerated. Harrison never carried out
his threat.

Today we were unlucky, but remember we only have to
be lucky once.
—From a statement made by the Irish Republican Army (IRA) after a bomb exploded
in the hotel where the British Prime Minister Margaret Thatcher and her cabinet were
staying in 1984. Four people were killed in the blast, which was clearly intended for
Mrs. Thatcher.

You had better put me to death, because next time it
might be one of you or your daughter.
—Steven Judy, multiple killer sentenced to death in 1980 for murdering an Indiana
woman and her three children, addressing the jury at his trial.

I know who you are, greaseball. And if you don't get back to the end of that fucking line, I'm gonna know who you *were*.
—James Lucas, Texas bank robber and fellow inmate of mobster Al Capone at Alcatraz, telling Capone to return to the end of the line as they were waiting for their monthly haircuts.

Those who refuse obedience to the orders of this secret society, or reveal its mysteries die by the dagger without mercy.
—Giuseppe Mazzini, organizer of the Young Italy Society, a society committed to terrorism and assassination which was the precursor of the Mafia.

We are not interested in cutting up your son piece by piece. We are not sadists. We are sending this letter to show the shame of this family which is the richest in the world. . . . If the family does not pay according to our conditions we will send another piece of him.
—Attributed to Sera Mommolitti, underboss in the Piromalli Mafia family, and Domenico Barbino, also of the Piromalli family, from the ransom note attached to the severed right ear of John Paul Getty III, grandson of billionaire John Paul Getty.

We want no more playing around. If you don't do what we say, you will get shot in the head.
—Frank "The Enforcer" Nitti, a henchman for Al Capone, informing a union leader of the possible consequences if the Capone gang wasn't allowed to put one of its own men in the union leadership.

If your uncle thinks he's going to put pizza in Eddie Arcaro's [restaurant] he's better off putting pizza in Scarpaci's, because that's where he's going to wind up.
—Frank "Funzi" Tieri, New York City-based mob boss, to Joe Cantalupo, regarding Cantalupo's uncle, who wanted to sell pizza in Eddie Arcaro's Restaurant, which was located in the same shopping complex as a pizza parlor owned by a relative of Tieri's. Scarpaci's is a funeral home.

timing

Then I got angry with her.
—Eben Gossage, drug addict, stating how he felt *after* he had bludgeoned his sister to death with 17 blows from a hammer.

It's too early to thank God!
—Ignaty Grinevitsky, an engineering student, responding to a voice in the crowd of people surrounding Czar Alexander II that shouted, "Thank God the czar is saved!" after an assassination attempt. Grinevitsky followed his statement by throwing a bomb which mortally wounded Alexander. More than 20 other people were killed in the blast, including Grinevitsky.

I only do my lady killing on Saturday night, fellas.
—Earle Leonard Nelson, a.k.a. "The Gorilla Murderer," mass murderer who killed women and then raped their corpses, when asked by police if he knew anything about the rash of murders in 1927.

They're just a mob. If I'd been there with my mob I could have taken over, just like they did. But over here, the time isn't ripe yet.
—Dutch Schultz, a.k.a Arthur Flegenheimer, New York mobster, comparing himself to the Bolsheviks.

too little too late

I've shot my husband. Come right over and help me. I don't know what to do.
—Janet Faye Carroll, in a phone conversation with her lover, after shooting her husband with a rifle.

My husband wants you urgently.
—Yvonne Chevallier, on the phone to the police after killing her husband, French politician Pierre Chevallier, by shooting him five times.

I'm very sorry for what has happened. I'm a good guy. I've been misconstrued.
—Vince Coleman, professional baseball player, apologizing for throwing a firecracker at baseball fans and injuring a two-year-old girl.

tough

I'll dance to your music all night.
—James Daly, a member of "Three-Fingered Jack" McDowell's Old West Nevada gang, drawing his gun and yelling to a man who had just shot him in the leg.

truth

I won't be home for a long time. . . .
—William Liebscher, Jr., a Florida car salesman who moonlighted as a bank robber, speaking to his wife after his arrest. He was sentenced to 15 years in prison.

undercover

I'm a big, farmer-ish looking sort of fellow, sort of easy going, like to laugh and talk and be chummy with people, and that doesn't match up with their ideas about criminals. And I always liked nice things—went to good shows, stayed at the best hotels, ate at the best places, and was always quiet and gentlemanly about it. People think crooks hide in cellars.

—Edward Wilhelm Bentz, notorious bank robber who left the circus as a teenager to embark upon a life of crime, on how he avoided being suspected of crimes.

understatement

It ain't nothin' officer. Rosie here ain't as dainty as she could be. . . . [She was making a] pig of herself. I tol' her not wipe her nose wit da tablecloth. Manners is important! Anyway, I only give her a little poke, just enough to put a shanty on her glimmer. But I always take off me knucks first.

—Edward "Monk" Eastman, a.k.a. Edward Osterman, New York City crime boss of the late-19th and early-20th centuries, to a police officer, after beating up a prostitute.

I like to read.

—Joseph Feldman, New York City resident whose apartment was found to house over 15,000 books from the New York Public Library, when asked why he stole the books.

upward mobility

I continuously grew.

—Sammy "The Bull" Gravano, henchman under Mafia don John Gotti who admitted killing 19 people, when asked about his stature in the family.

You start stealing and you see how it reaches around, and you try to advance yourself. You see the next man in the rackets go higher and higher, and you want to go higher, too. Everybody wants to get ahead in the world. Well, we also want to advance ourselves higher and higher.

—Abe Reles, a paid killer for Murder, Inc., confessing to the Brooklyn district attorney.

victory

They were dead and I was alive. That was the victory in
my case.
—Edmund Emil Kemper III, a California man who murdered eight people, speaking about
his victims.

wages

$250 a head for policemen! You kill a cop, I give
you $250 right away. Just make sure you kill him, not
just hurt him. He never gets up again. Dead. All of
them, dead.
—Rosario Borgio, the Akron, Ohio, Mafia don who couldn't corrupt the police force
and so ordered the murder of its policemen. His henchmen did in fact kill some policemen, but ultimately Borgio himself was killed—in the electric chair.

warnings

My love (as things stand today) is for the South alone.
Nor do I deem it a dishonor in attempting to make for
her a prisoner of this man [Lincoln], to whom she owes
so much misery.
—John Wilkes Booth, actor who assassinated President Abraham Lincoln in 1865, from
a letter a few months before the assassination.

Don't go to sleep 'cause I'm going to kill you.
—Ricky Briscoe, before dousing his girlfriend with kerosene and setting her on fire,
burning her to death.

Next time I will cut that wagging tongue out completely!
—Elizabeth Brownrigg, 18th-century midwife, speaking to a servant girl whose tongue
she had just slashed with a scissor. Brownrigg later beat the girl to death.

If you are unable to go at your time, it will be necessary
to wait until the next day when your turn comes again.
—John Cammillieri, a Mafia henchman, in his message to workers at a construction
site regarding time allotted for toilet breaks.

I bite.
—Jeffrey Dahmer, serial killer and cannibal, to his jail guards.

Come prepared to stay forever.
—Belle Gunness, Indiana woman who lured men to her farm by either placing ads in newspapers or writing them love letters, one of which ended with the line above. She then drugged, robbed, murdered, butchered, and buried the men, killing 14 in all.

Compare, be aware that we don't like crooked things.
—Paolo Violi, Italian-born heir to the Cotroni crime family who was sentenced to jail for contempt of court, to someone who had used his name without permission.

whining

It ain't fair, my reputation is being used against me.
—Elmer "Trigger" Burke, robber and freelance killer, complaining during his murder trial.

He called me a fat scumbag motherfucker, Judge . . . .
—Giacomo "Fat Jack" DiNorscio, mobster who acted as his own counsel during his drug trafficking trial, complaining to the judge about a federal prosecutor.

Here I am, helping the government, helping my country, and that little son of a bitch is breaking my balls.
—Johnny Roselli, Mafia hit man who claimed he was hired by President John F. Kennedy to assassinate Cuban leader Fidel Castro, while Bobby Kennedy, the United States attorney general and brother of the president, was in the midst of a campaign to eradicate the Mafia.

I am a cripple and must be armed to put me on fair terms with others. . . . I have an absolute right to kill.
—Bernard Hugh Walden, lecturer at a technical college in England, who shot and killed the woman who spurned him. He also killed her boyfriend.

why

She was just too pushy.
—Robert Chambers, a.k.a. "The Preppie Murderer," on why he strangled his prep school classmate to death.

I just wanted to make it an even fifty.
—Edward "Monk" Eastman, a.k.a. Edward Osterman, New York City crime boss of the late-19th and early-20th centuries, on why he beat a man unconscious. Eastman carried a knife, the handle of which was marked with notches for each of his victims.

I cannot get the smell of her decaying body out of my system.
—Derrick Edwardson, Briton who murdered a four-year-old girl, giving his reason for turning himself in to the police.

I had not seen the woman before in my life and had not the least ill intentions toward her. I just murdered her because I wanted to murder someone.
—Frederick Field, English airman who strangled a woman to death, confessing his crime to the authorities.

The old fool! I wanted her to give me some money—it was the only way I could get it.
—Louis Fine, murderer who strangled his landlady to death in order to inherit her money immediately; she had already named him as sole beneficiary.

It's about lack of balls.
—Joe N. Gallo, consigliere of the Gambino crime family, on why someone would ask the Mafia for help on a strong-arm job, i.e. on a job someone wouldn't have the guts to do for himself.

. . . And I sat with this guy. I saw the papers and every thing. He didn't rob nothin'! You know why he's dying? He's gonna die because he refused to come in when I called. He didn't do nothin' else wrong.
—John Gotti, boss of the Gambino crime family.

For no reason at all, I raised the knife and let her have it. I don't know why, but I let her have it.
—Rodney Greig, confessing to the murder of his girlfriend, who he stabbed to death outside Oakland, California, in 1938.

The reason Islam has put so many people to death [is] to insure the safety of Moslem peoples and their interests.
—Ayatollah Ruhollah Khomeini, virtual dictator of Iran during the 1970s and '80s.

. . . I thought buried men cannot bear witness, so I shot him, with his wife and lodger.
—Kuznetsof, Russian criminal who murdered six people, on the killing of his uncle.

That's why I choked these ladies. It was to get their voices!
—Edward Joseph Leonski, Texas man who killed three women while serving with the army in Australia in 1942.

I don't have time for a wife.
—Charles "Lucky" Luciano, mobster-founder of the national crime syndicate, who was found guilty of dozens of prostitution-related crimes, on why he was a customer of two madams.

I . . . do things for my own dignity.
—Giacomo Luppino, don of the Hamilton, Ontario, mob, from a wiretapped conversation, on why he runs his operation ruthlessly.

I must have gone out of my mind. It was something in me that exploded.
—Patrick Mackay, 23-year-old psychopathic killer, on the murder of a priest.

. . . . Take the first one I killed for instance. . . . I had to change his bed clothes several times a day and I got tired of it.
—Frederick Mors, a porter at a home for the elderly, who poisoned 17 of its inhabitants from 1914 to 1915.

Besides, I never killed a kid before. I wanted to see how it felt.
—Stephen Nash, California drifter turned murderer, on why he murdered a 10-year-old.

I was tired of being her slave boy.
—Marvin Pancoast, a Hollywood hanger-on, telling why he beat to death his apartment mate, Vicki Morgan, the mistress of department store magnate Alfred Bloomingdale. The trial revealed Bloomingdale and Morgan's participation in sadomasochistic orgies.

I killed him because he made a fool of me.
—Angelina Testro, who stalked her would-be husband to death because he demanded $400 from her in order to go through with the marriage.

wishes

Would that the Roman people had but one neck.
—Gaius Caesar Caligula, first-century Roman emperor.

I don't want to die, shot down in the street like an animal.
—Al Capone, legendary mobster who controlled Chicago during the 1920s and '30s. His wish was granted; he died of syphilis.

wishful thinking

I suppose it's too much to hope that you gentleman are burglars?
—Robert Augustus Delaney, British robber known as the first "cat burglar," upon being surprised by the police while he was resting at home.

women

The bitch set me up.
—Marion Barry, Washington, DC, mayor, surprised at being caught on videotape smoking crack.

**I am deeply hurt by your calling me a weman-hater [sic].
I am not. But I am a monster. I am the Son of Sam. I
am a little brat. . . . I love to hunt, prowling the streets,
looking for fair game . . . tasty meat . . . . The weman
[sic] of Queens are the prettyist of all.**
—David Berkowitz, a.k.a. "The Son of Sam," paranoid killer who shot 14 people and
terrorized New York City between 1975 and 1977, in a note found at one of the murder sites.

**The German girl is a subject and only becomes a citizen
when she marries.**
—Adolf Hitler in *Mein Kampf.*

**Her voice was sweet and soft, and I could feel myself
going mad about it.**
—Edward Joseph Leonski, a Texas GI serving in Australia when he murdered three
women, explaining the motivation for one of the murders he committed.

What I did is not such a great harm with all these surplus women nowadays. Anyway, I had a good time.
—Rudolf Pleil, a German man convicted of nine rape/murders, but who claimed to have committed 25.
He called himself Germany's "champion death maker."

My harem takes me to several places.
—Alfred Arthur Rouse, a traveling salesman who had as many as 80 affairs and was
guilty of bigamy, speaking to the police. Rouse also picked up a stranger and then
killed him by setting his car on fire.

**The German woman enthusiastically fights at the führer's
side in his battle for the universal recognition of the
German race and German culture.**
—Gertrud Scholtz-Klink, Nazi Women's League leader of the Third Reich.

[You are] a reward for [my] friends.
—Tupac Shakur, considered by many to be the king of "Gangsta Rap," to a woman he
forced to perform oral sex on three of his friends. He was convicted of sexual abuse.

I can't stand a bitchy chick.
—Gerald Eugene Stano, mass murderer who may have killed 40 women on why
he murdered.

Man, I'll never forget that punch. It was when I fought
with Robin in Steve's apartment. She really offended me
and I went bam, and she flew backward, hitting every
wall in the apartment. That was the best punch I've ever
thrown in my fucking life.
—Mike Tyson, heavyweight champion boxer who was convicted of raping a beauty
pageant contestant, on beating his wife at the time, Robin Givens.

wrong

I consider myself a normal, average girl.
—Penny Bjorkland, an 18-year-old who murdered a gardener "just to see if [she] could,
and not worry about it afterwards."

. . . Deputy Blunk says I had a real .45 that's just a lot
of hooey to cover up because they don't like to admit
that I locked eight deputys [sic] and a dozen trustys
[friends] up with my wooden gun before I got my hands
on the two machine guns and you should have seen their
faces. Ha! Ha! Ha! Don't part with my wooden gun for
any price. For when you feel blue all you have to do is
look at the gun and laugh your blues away. Ha! Ha!
—John Dillinger, infamous bank robber of the 1920s and '30s, from a letter to his
sister. Dillinger had recently escaped from jail with a fake gun he had carved out
of wood.

Mr. Ferguson was awakened by the gunfire and, amid the confusion, sought to protect himself.
—Colin Ferguson, proclaiming his innocence. Ferguson had shot 26 people on the Long Island Rail Road,
killing six, in front of dozens of witnesses.

No one will ever kill me—they wouldn't dare.
—Carmine Galante, a.k.a. "Mr. Lilo," mobster in the Bonnano crime family. Four days
later he was shot to death by four men weilding shotguns.

We shall go down in history as the greatest statesmen of
all time, or as the greatest criminals.
—Joseph Goebbels, Nazi Propaganda Minister.

I have slain the Antichrist!
—Guseva, a prostitute, after stabbing the licentious Russian religious figure Grigory
Yefimovich Rasputin; Rasputin lived.

I am completely normal. Even while I was carrying out the task of extermination I lived a normal life and so on.
—Rudolf Hess, Nazi commandant of the concentration and extermination camp at
Auschwitz, from his autobiography.

These assholes will never get me.
—Philip Leonetti, underboss of the Bruno/Scarfo crime family, speaking about the authorities. He was soon charged with 10 murders and five attempted murders, and was
ultimately sentenced to 45 years in prison.

I have absolute power [because of the] complete trust of my people for me and vice-versa.
—Mohammad-Reza Pahlavi, the Shah of Iran, who organized Savak, a brutal secret
police renowned for its torture techniques.

Gaiety is the most outstanding feature of the Soviet Union.
—Joseph Stalin, Soviet political leader.

The Bolsheviks will hang you one day!
—Julius Streicher, Nazi administrator tried at Nuremberg, Germany, as he fell through the trap door at
his hanging in 1946.

youthful pursuits

It's been a childhood dream to rape a girl. . . . I have always wanted to kill.
—Thomas Lee Bean, Reno, Nevada, man who murdered and dismembered a woman
in 1963.

It seems as if I always had a piece of rope in my hand when I was a kid.
—Harvey Murray Glatman, strangler who posed as a photographer in order to lure three
women to him and then murder them, recalling how he excelled at knot tying when he
was in the Boy Scouts.

It all started when I stole a fruit from a truck in my neighborhood. . . . You could not believe how this fucking guy chased me for a goddamned fruit. You would think if a kid is hungry just left [sic] him take it, but this fucking Puerto Rican man was on my tail for a long time, just for a fucking fruit. After a few blocks he gave up and I was saying to myself, "What the hell are you doing, man, chasing me for so long for a fucking fruit?"

—Mike Tyson, heavyweight champion boxer convicted of rape, on the beginnings of his juvenile thievery.

sources

The following is an abridged list of major sources used to compile this book. Additional biographies, autobiographies, histories, newspapers, and periodicals were also consulted.

Balsamo, William. *Crime Incorporated: The Inside Story of the Mafia's First Hundred Years*. True Crime, 1993.

Barnhart, Joe E. *Jim and Tammy: Charismatic Intrigue Inside PTL*. Prometheus Books, 1989.

Blumenthal, Ralph. *Last Days of the Sicilians: At War with the Mafia; the FBI Assault on the Pizza Connection*. Times Books, 1988.

Bonanno, Joseph, with Sergio Lalli. *A Man of Honor: The Autobiography of Joseph Bonanno*. Simon & Schuster, 1983.

Brashler, William. *The Don: The Life and Death of Sam Giancana*. Harper & Row, 1977.

Bugliosi, Vincent, with Curt Gentry. *Helter Skelter: The True Story of the Manson Murders*. W. W. Norton, 1974.

Chandler, David Leon. *Brothers in Blood: The Rise of the Criminal Brotherhoods*. Dutton, 1975.

Davis, John H. *Mafia Dynasty: The Rise and Fall of the Gambino Crime Family.* HarperCollins, 1993.

Edwards, Peter. *Blood Brothers: How Canada's Most Powerful Mafia Family Runs Its Business.* Key Porter Books, 1990.

English, T. J. *Born to Kill: America's Most Notorious Vietnamese Gang, and the Changing Face of Organized Crime.* William Morrow, 1995.

Fisher, Amy, with Sheila Weller. *Amy Fisher, My Story.* Pocket Books, 1993.

Fox, Stephen R. *Blood and Power: Organized Crime in Twentieth-Century America.* William Morrow, 1989.

Fresolone, George, with Robert J. Wagman. *Blood Oath: The Heroic Story of a Gangster Turned Government Agent Who Brought Down One of America's Most Powerful Mob Families.* Simon & Schuster, 1994.

Gaute, J. H. H., and Robin Odell. *The New Murderer's Who's Who.* Harrap, 1989.

Haley, J. Evetts. *Robbing Banks Was My Business: The Story of J. Harvey Bailey, America's Most Successful Bank Robber.* Palo Duro Press, 1973.

Handelman, Stephen. *Comrade Criminal: Russia's New Mafiya.* Yale University Press, 1995.

Iannuzzi, Joseph. *The Mafia Cookbook.* Simon & Schuster, 1993.

King, Martin, and Marc Breault. *Preacher of Death: The Shocking Inside Story of David Koresh and the Waco Siege.* Penguin, 1993.

Lacey, Robert. *Little Man: Meyer Lansky and the Gangster Life.* Little, Brown & Co., 1991.

Leyton, Elliott. *Hunting Humans.* McClelland & Stewart, 1986.

Maas, Peter. *Killer Spy: The Inside Story of the FBI's Pursuit and Capture of Aldrich Ames, America's Deadliest Spy.* Warner Books, 1995.

McKinley, James. *Assassination in America.* Harper & Row, 1977.

Meader, Thomas. *The Unspeakable Crimes of Dr. Petiot.* Little, Brown & Co., 1980.

Melady, Thomas Patrick. *Idi Amin Dada: Hitler in Africa.* Sheed, Andrews, and McMeel, 1977.

Moquin, Wayne, with Charles Van Doren. *The American Way of Crime: A Documentary History.* Praeger, 1976.

Mustain, Gene, and Jerry Capeci. *Mob Star: The Story of John Gotti.* F. Watts, 1988.

Nash, Jay Robert. *Bloodletters and Badmen.* M. Evans & Co., 1991.

———. *Crime Chronology.* Facts on Filc, 1984.

———. *Encyclopedia of World Crime.* Paragon House, 1992.

———. *Hustlers and Con Men: An Anecdotal History of the Confidence Man and His Games.* M. Evans & Co., 1976.

———. *Look for the Woman.* M. Evans & Co., 1981

Nelli, Humbert S. *The Business of Crime: Italians and Syndicate Crime in the United States.* Oxford University Press, 1976.

Newton, Michael. *Hunting Humans: An Encyclopedia of Modern Serial Killers.* Loompanics Unlimited, 1990.

Nicolle, David. *The Mongol Warlords: Genghis Khan, Kublai Khan, Hulegu, Tamerlane.* Firebird, 1990.

O'Brien, Joseph. *Boss of Bosses: The Fall of the Godfather.* Simon & Schuster, 1991.

Olive, David. *Political Babble.* John Wiley & Sons, 1992.

Rudolph, Robert. *The Boys from New Jersey: How the Mob Beat the Feds.* William Morrow, 1992.

Shawcross, Tim. *The War Against the Mafia.* Mainstream, 1994.

————, and Martin Young. *Men of Honour: The Confessions of Tommaso Buscetta.* Collins, 1987.

Short, Martin. *Crime Inc.: The Story of Organized Crime.* Thames Methuen, 1994.

Sifakis, Carl. *The Encyclopedia of American Crime.* Facts on File, 1982.

————. *The Encyclopedia of Assassinations.* Headline, 1993.

————. *The Mafia Encyclopedia.* Facts on File, 1987.

Teresa, Vincent Charles, with Thomas C. Renner. *My Life in the Mafia.* Doubleday, 1973.

Tidwell, Gary. *Anatomy of a Fraud: Inside the Finances of the PTL Ministries.* John Wiley & Sons, 1993.

Time-Life Books, ed. *Crimes of Passion.* Time-Life Books, 1994.

———. *Crimes and Punishments.* Time-Life Books, 1994.

Waldo, Gordon P. *Career Criminals.* Sage, 1983.

Watson, Charles, with Ray Chaplain. *Will You Die for Me?* F. H. Revell, 1978.

Weiner, Tim, with Tim Johnston and Neil A. Lewis. *Betrayal: The Story of Aldrich Ames, An American Spy.* Random House, 1995.

Weyermann, Debra. *The Gang They Couldn't Catch: The Story of America's Greatest Modern-Day Bank Robbers—And How They Got Away with It.* Simon & Schuster, 1993.

Wistrich, Robert S. *Who's Who in Nazi Germany.* Macmillan, 1982.

Wolfe, Linda. *Wasted: The Preppie Murderer.* Simon & Schuster, 1989.

index

Betty Broderick
129
California homemaker who shot and killed her ex-husband along with his new wife.

Louis Dwight Brookins
16
Lured young women to desolate areas in order to kill them.

Leo Vincent Brothers
7
St. Louis killer hired by mobster Al Capone to kill newsman Jake Lingle in 1930.

James Brown
(a.k.a. "The Godfather of Soul")
56
Singer arrested for criminal domestic violence.

Sam Brown
30
Outlaw gunman of the Nevada mining camps of the 1850s, who reportedly killed 15 men.

Thomas Mathieson Brown
50
Sent strychnine-laced cake to his wife's elderly uncle and killed his housekeeper.

Elizabeth Brownrigg
133
18th-century midwife who slashed her servant's tongue and later beat the girl to death.

Charles Bryant
(a.k.a. "Black Face Charlie")
45, 99
Late-19th-century bandit.

Fiore "Fifi" Buccieri
44
Personal hit man for Mafia boss Sam Giancana and the Chicago Syndicate.

Russell A. Bufalino
38
Boss of the Pittstown, Pennsylvania, crime family.

David Bullock
54
Street hustler who killed a man

because he was "messing with the Christmas tree."

Ted Bundy
50, 62
Serial killer.

Elmer "Trigger" Burke
134
Robber and freelance killer.

Tommaso Buscetta
118, 121
Sicilian Mafia leader.

Joey Buttafuoco
59, 117, 118
Long Island, New York, mechanic turned tabloid TV regular, who was convicted of statutory rape, pled no contest to attempting to solicit a prostitute, and was accused of encouraging his under-age girlfriend, Amy Fisher, a.k.a. "The Long Island Lolita," to shoot his wife.

Kitty Byron
103
23-year-old British woman who stabbed her lover to death.

Henriette Caillaux
99
Wife of France's Minister of Finance Joseph Caillaux; she shot to death an editor of *Le Figaro* after they published several negative editorials about her husband.

Gaius Caesar Caligula
55, 58, 98, 105, 136
First-century, criminally insane, Roman emperor with a taste for orgies and senseless killings.

John Cammillieri
62, 64, 133
Mafia henchman.

Louis "Little New York" Campagna
114
Al Capone's bodyguard and hit man for the Chicago Syndicate during the 1920s and '30s.

Joseph "Joey" Cantalupo
116

Nazi and Luftwaffe commander in chief. Under heavy guard, he mysteriously took his own life while imprisoned during the Trials at Nuremberg.

Bernhard H. Goetz
54, 87
Electrical engineering consultant called the "Subway Vigilante," who shot three of the four men he claimed were going to rob him on a New York City subway car in 1984.

Crawford Goldsby
(a.k.a. "Cherokee Bill")
46
Outlaw robber and gunman who killed 13 men.

Arthur Frederick Goode III
119
Infamous child molester.

Anthony Goodin
88
Drifter who murdered a Georgia schoolteacher.

Harry W. Gordon
23, 54
Morgue janitor turned murderer.

Waxey Gordon
23, 91
One of the biggest Prohibition-era bootleggers, who eventually was jailed on income tax evasion charges. After his release he went into narcotics trafficking.

Eben Gossage
130
Drug addict who bludgeoned his sister to death.

John Gotti
2, 18, 42, 56, 65, 66, 73, 86, 98, 103, 129, 132, 135
Gambino crime family boss, ultimately convicted of racketeering and murder.

Janice Gould
49
Helped kill her boss, an optometrist, with the help of his wife.

Hans Graewe
(a.k.a. "The Surgeon")

56, 75
Hit man for a Cleveland, Ohio, gang who was well-known for his expertise at cutting up bodies.

John "Jack" Gilbert Graham
20, 46, 57
Sabotaged the plane flight his mother was on, killing 43 others in the process.

Sammy "The Bull" Gravano
132
Mafia don John Gotti's henchman, who admitted killing 19 people.

Giuseppe "Pino" Greco
53
Bloodthirsty Mafioso whose passion was the supervision of executions.

Rodney Greig
135
Stabbed his girlfriend to death.

Irma Grese
126
Sadistic, murderous Nazi concentration camp supervisor.

Peter Griffiths
28
Briton who kidnapped and killed a four-year-old girl.

Martha Grinder
28
19th-century Pittsburgh woman who slowly poisoned her neighbor to death.

Ignaty Grinevitsky
131
In a bombing attatck, assassinated Czar Alexander II, killing himself and more than 20 others in the process.

Maria Groesbeek
28
South African who used insect poison to kill her husband.

Herbie Gross
63
Front man and hotel owner for the Mafia turned federal witness.

Charles Guiteau
32
Assassin of President James A. Garfield.